AF304962

ROBERT ALAN JAMIESON was born in Lerwick on
Up Helly Aa, 1958 and grew up in the crofting
community of Sandness. He attended the University
of Edinburgh as a mature student and subsequently
held the William Soutar Fellowship in Perth. He was
a co-editor of *Edinburgh Review,* 1993–98, and
writer in residence at the Universities of Glasgow
and Strathclyde, 1998–2001. Since then he has
tutored creative writing at the University of
Edinburgh. He is the author of three novels,
two collections of poetry and two plays, and has
edited a number of anthologies. Through his
occasional work with the organisation Literature
Across Frontiers, his poetry in Shetlandic Scots has
been translated into more than a dozen languages,
and he has translated over 20 contemporary
European poets into Shetlandic Scots.

Nort Atlantik Drift

Poyims ati'Shætlin
Translations and Commentary in English

ROBERT ALAN JAMIESON

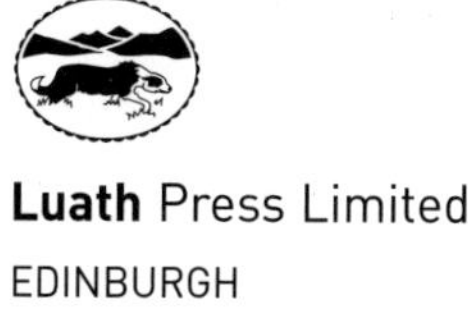

Luath Press Limited

EDINBURGH

www.luath.co.uk

First published 2007

ISBN (10): 1-906307-13-X

ISBN (13): 978-1-906307-13-4

The paper used in this book is recyclable. It is made
from low chlorine pulps produced in a low energy,
low emission manner from renewable forests.

The author's right to be identified as author of this book
under the Copyright, Designs and Patents Act 1988 has
been asserted.

The publisher acknowledges the support of

 Scottish **Arts** Council

towards the publication of this volume.

Published by Luath Press
Printed and bound by CPI Antony Rowe, Chippenham
Designed by Tom Bee
Typeset by 3btype.com

© Robert Alan Jamieson 2007

Dis wark is dediekætit t'da aald fokk a'Saanis'at
gied me mie first edjukæsjin:

da Huxter fokk

da Snösquhie fokk

da Melville fokk

da Punds fokk

da Brekk fokk

da Brekknamyrs fokk

da fokk a'da Waast Striet

da Krakk fokk

da Mukkil Haa fokk

da Aald Haa fokk

da Saands fokk

da fokk a'da Æst Striet

da Blikk fokk

da Sillerdæks fokk

da Sillerførd fokk

da Wast Gærdiens fokk

da Æst Gærdiens fokk

da Know fokk

da Kruisdæl fokk

da Quhisillbær fokk

da Lamtoon fokk

da Goshiegill fokk

da Houll fokk

da fokk a'Noarbie

da Windiehill fokk

da Langhill fokk

da Turriefield fokk

da Forrits fokk

da Millhaagh fokk

da Goard fokk

da Niep fokk

da Gert fokk

da Kollaster fokk

da Kratoon fokk

da Myrs fokk

da fokk a'da Ness

da Littla Boosta fokk

da Boosta fokk

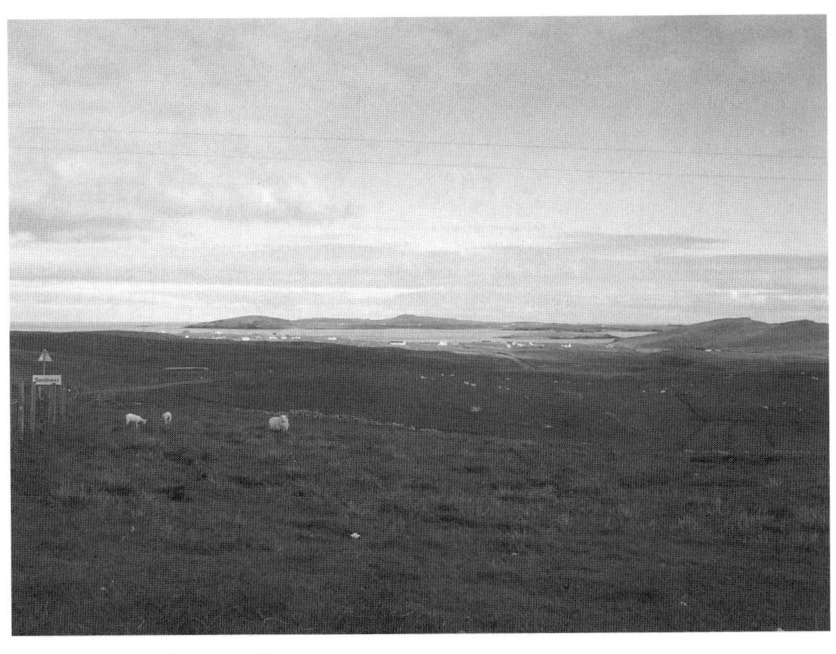
Sandness

Contents

III ATLANTIK MARIEN

ACKNOWLEDGEMENTS

A number of these poems have appeared in *Briggistanes*, *The New Shetlander*, *Stand*, *Chapman*, *Gown*, HEAT (Australia) and *Lallans* magazines.

A selection was published in *Ahead of its Time* (Cape 1997) edited by Duncan McLean, and in *Wish I Was Here* (pocketbooks 2000) edited by Kevin MacNeil and Alec Finlay.

The author gratefully acknowledges the support of the Scottish Arts Council while working on this project, in the form of a Writers Bursary awarded in 1997.

The author would also like to thank Murdo Macdonald and Jack Jamieson for their contributions. Photographs taken by Murdo Macdonald appear on pages 46 and 47. Photographs taken by Jack Jamieson appear on pages 17, 95, 107 and 119.

NOTES

TEXT: The first and last poems in this book were both written in Shetland in 1987 but remained otherwise unconnected until June 1994, when I attended the Portsoy Small Boats Festival. This event gave birth to the concept of a sequence of maritime poems stretching between these 'poles' – the first pure autobiography and the last pure fiction. The rest followed over the next two years, developing as a kind of 'life-I-might-have-led', had the nine-year-old boy I was gone to sea as he thought he might.

Originally I thought these poems were for my three sons, a record of who their father had firstly been and who he once thought he might be – at the time of writing, in the mid-90s, they were growing up far from Shetland and far from the sea. But as with life, the narrative developed in ways I didn't foresee. The sequence departed from autobiography somewhere in the middle and became an act of retrieval for me of a way of life I had witnessed, rather than experienced – that of the merchant seamen.

The poems as first written were in a form which, on reflection, seemed to me to make too many concessions to standard English, given the focus was mainly on the world of my childhood on the west coast of Shetland in the 1960s, among a community of 'Shætlin' (what linguists call 'Modern Shetlandic Scots') speakers. So I began to create dual-language text. With this approach I felt I could show something of the unique dialect of my village at that time, while the English prose translations and notes could open the meaning of the poems to readers who didn't share my origins, or had no understanding of the local word-stock, the unusual grammatical forms, or the presence of so-called 'Scandinavian vowels'. To render the last visually, I make use of symbols common in Scandinavian alphabets. Similarly, certain consonants are represented by non-English forms. The product may at first appear strange, yet there is a relatively consistent and simple orthographic system to this work which I hope goes some distance towards representing a unique shoot of the Germanic tree of language in script form; a linguistic time-capsule where Nordic meets Anglic. A fuller explanation of the orthography adopted appears in my essay 'A Quite-Right upon the Sacred Peatbank' (2004), available from the Scottish Poetry Library.

As I've read these poems over the last 12 or 20 years – to audiences in Shetland and abroad, from Tallinn to Bilbao, Tel Aviv to Ouessant – so each poem has accrued a brief preamble: a portal for listening strangers. In Prague or Perth, even living beside an ocean requires a gloss. These portals have become a part of the work, and form the basis of the commentary here.

SOUND: This book has an audio-visual counterpart featuring recordings I made of the *Nort Atlantik Drift* poems in 2006, synchronized with photographs reproduced here and others. The AV show is primarily designed for projection, but a CD for computers is available from the Scottish Poetry Library. Downloads of these recordings are available from www.robertalanjamieson.info

IMAGE: The cover photograph of fish drying on a washing line, taken by my good friend Murdo Macdonald outside Captain Peter Peterson's house at Melby in 1992, is the single image that inspired the idea of combining a visual aspect with these poems. The bulk of the others date from the last five years, and in the main portray Sandness and the south side of Saint Magnus Bay, with an occasional foray northwards to Eshaness and the rest of the 'da Nortlaand', but towards the middle of the sequence, as the poetic narrative wanders from those familiar shores, so too does the pictorial, ranging to other parts of Shetland, and finally beyond. The last photographs chronologically are those of *The Reaper*, a herring drifter that once sailed out of Scalloway in Shetland, and was at one time named *The Shetlander*. They were taken while she was moored in St Andrews' harbour during the StAnza poetry festival in March 2007, when the AV show of *Nort Atlantik Drift* played in her fo'c's'le for the weekend. Thanks to the crew for fitting it in – and to Ian Stephen for that great Cullen Skink.

Except where noted, images are mine.

RAJ 22.10.2007

I

ATLASLAAND

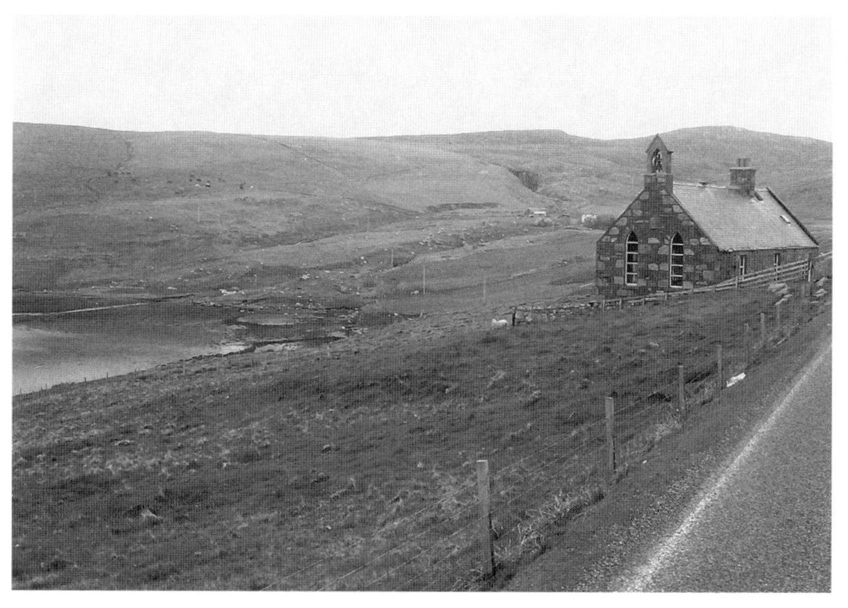

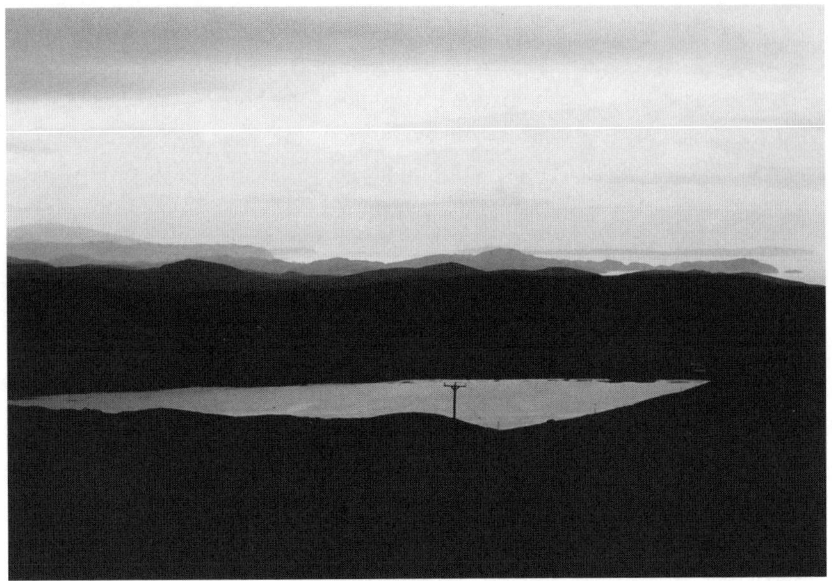

THE BOATBUILDER'S NEPHEW

Arthur Anderson, known as Alan, was my maternal uncle. As a young man he went to the Merchant Navy and the whaling in South Georgia. Over many years he built himself a boat for lobster fishing, but died suddenly, before he had time to get the full use of it. The family crofted land overlooking Gonfirth, a sheltered inlet at the centre of the island group, yet isolated by the road system. The poem is a gathering of fragments of memories from holidays and Sundays spent at my grandfather's house in Gonfirth, where a beautiful, mysterious sailing ship in a bottle and an outsize Readers' Digest *Great World Atlas* held great fascination.

DA BOAT BIGGIR'S NEFJOO

Quhan da bærns chap da windoo
he hadds up da sjip ati'da bottil,
sjaaks his hed – awa!

An da aald fokk sæ –
'Tink næthin o'it.'
'Tym'll tell.' 'Du'll fin dy nitch.'

He tinks – Foo dæs'it kum t'gjing insyd?
No a trikk, bit maachikk.
Dønna shaa me, I waant it ta happin.

An da aald fokk sæ –
'Quhar dir's a will, dir's a wy.
Aniddir skurtfoo fæ da skroo.'

He tinks – Nyntents o an ysberg's hoidit.
Ungkil Alan wis a quhælir.
Dær's da mukkil atlas a'da windoo.

An da aald fokk sæ –
'Du'll miss'it if du blinks.'
'Hadd tyght noo.' 'Dønna aks me, I dønna ken.'

Da njoo kaaf's brølin ati'da byr.
Da aald koo's rekkin trow da widdin slats –
A pæl a'jalloo mylk fir da jungstir.

An da aald fokk sæ –
'Heir da burn rush noo!' 'Ir da hens in?'
'We'll fieniesh it da moarn, Gød willin.'

An Mammie sæs – 'A'll læv de lyght a staart.
Pit by da book noo. Læjie up da Kuttie Sark.
Sall I tell de foo hit's don?'

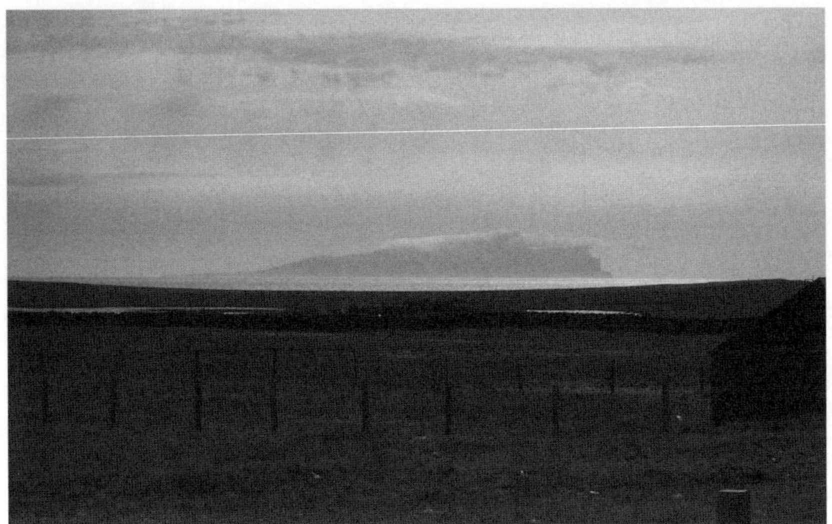

When the children tap the window, he holds up the ship in the bottle,
shakes his head – Away!

And the old folk say – 'Think nothing of it.' 'Time will tell.' 'You'll
find your niche.'

He thinks – How does it come to go inside? Not a trick, but magic.
Don't show me, I want it to happen.

And the old folk say – 'Where there's a will there's a way. Another
armful from the haystack.'

He thinks – Nine-tenths of an iceberg's hidden. Uncle Alan was a
whaler. There's the big atlas in the window.

And the old folks say – 'You'll miss it if you blink.' 'Hold tight now.'
'Don't ask me, I don't know.'

The new calf's crying in the byre. The old cow's tongue is reaching
through the slats. A pail of yellow milk for the youngster.

And the old folks say – 'Hear the stream rush now!' 'Are the hens in?'
'We'll finish it tomorrow, God willing.'

And Mammie says – 'I'll leave your light on a bit. Put the book aside.
Set up the Cutty Sark. Shall I tell you how it's done?'

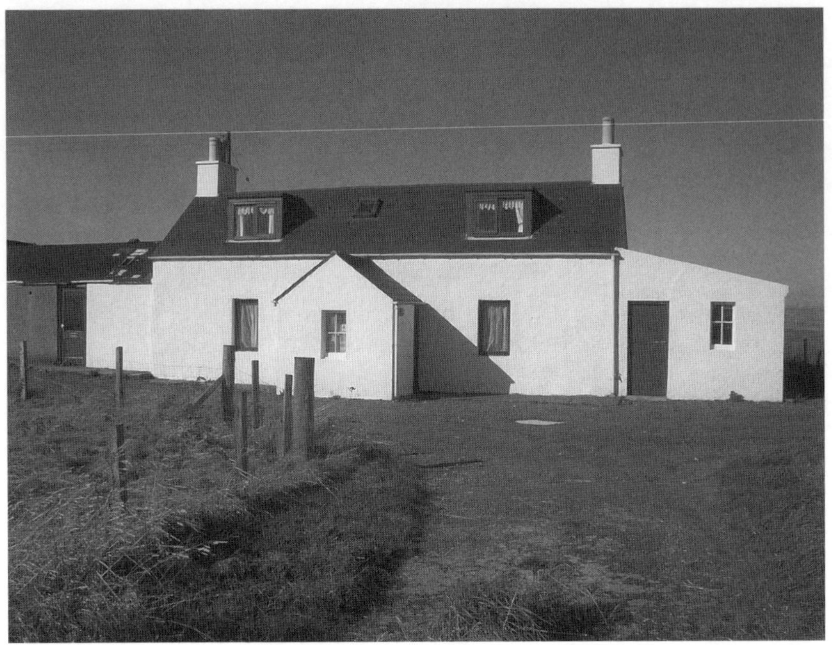

FRESH WATER TROUT

Fresh water lochs like Melby in Sandness were a playground for young fish and children, providing a sheltered place to learn the skills necessary for open waters. My older brother Peter kept a little 'flat-bottom' boat there, and on a fine day, 'Da Loch' was a favourite destination. The word 'frisk' has an interesting etymology, circumnavigating the North Sea, with comparatives in Old English 'fersc', meaning 'the opposite to salt'; Old French 'frisque' and Middle English 'fresshe', 'freche', 'fressche', meaning 'full of life and spirit'; Old Teutonic and Modern Norwegian share the word 'frisk', meaning 'fresh' and 'healthy'.

FRISK WAATIR TROOT

Afoar he lærns t'sykil a byk
he's tentilie rowin da flatboddim
roond an aroond Melbie logh.

Siks jieir aald
an dark pætie waatir's
slappin at da syd.

He's wurriet'at sumien myght kiek
fæ da quhyt-waasht hoos
akross da girssie mødoo an sie

waatir siepin in aboot
his rubbir bøt fiet –
an he'd gjit a lugfoo

quhan he wan hem,
fir no tellin oniebodie
he lækit denchir tø.

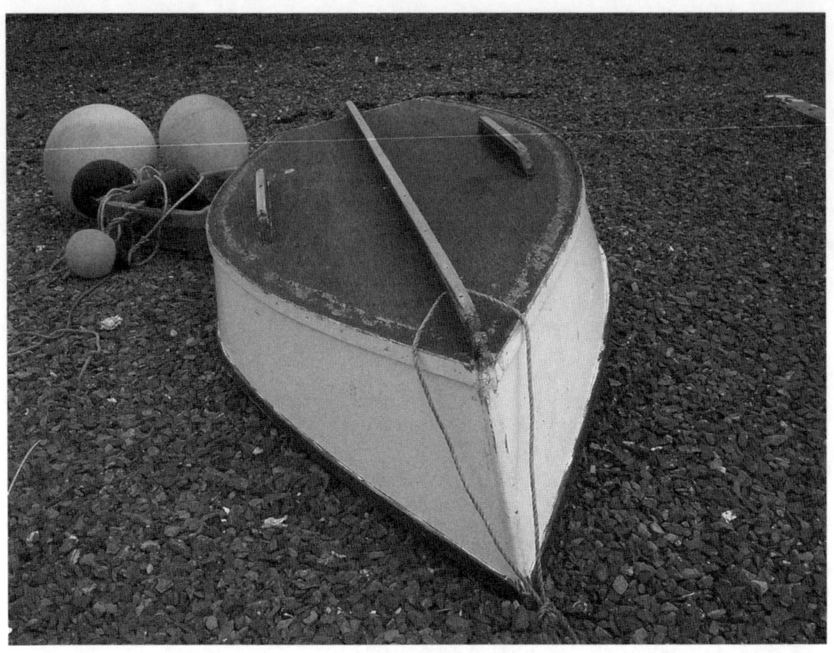

Before he learns to ride a bike, he's carefully rowing the skiff, round
and around Melby loch.

Six years old, and dark peaty water's slapping at the side.

He's worried that someone might look from the white-washed house
across the grassy meadow and see

Water seeping in about his rubber-boot feet – and he'd get an earful

When he got home, for not telling anybody that he likes danger too.

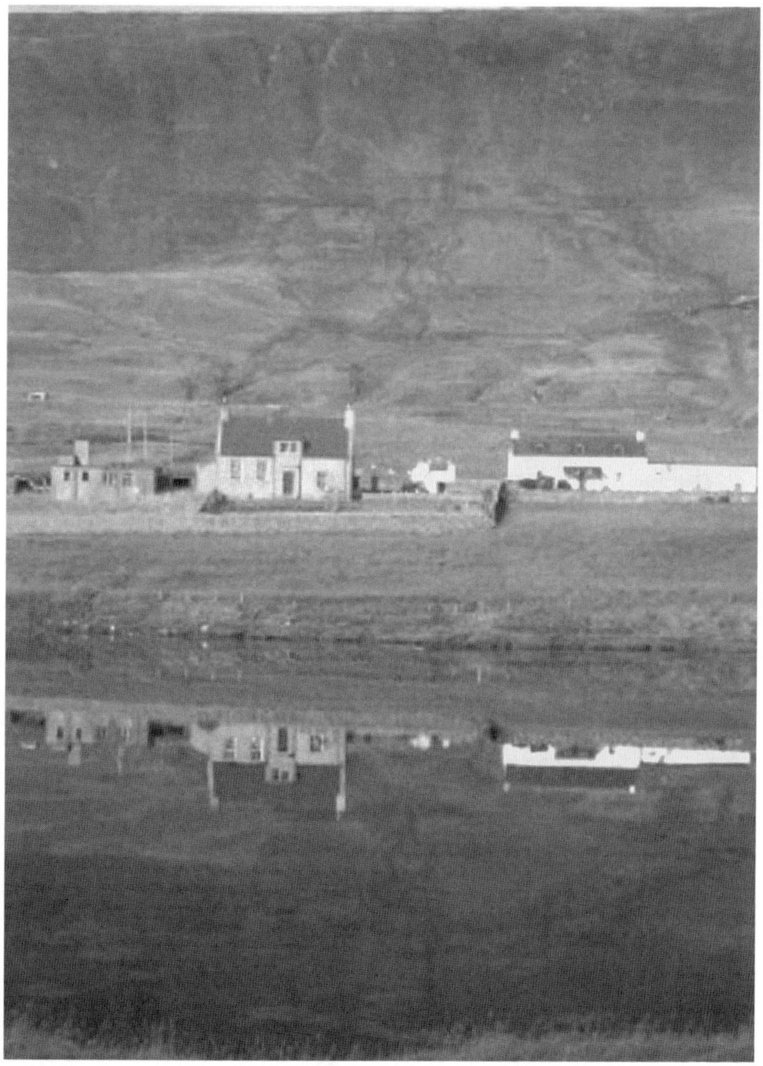

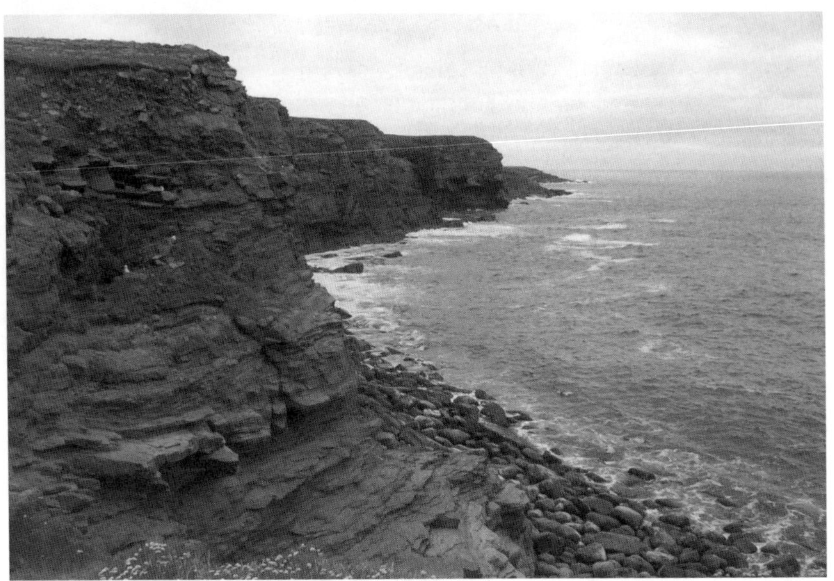

ATLANTIS

The legend of the lost continent believed to have lain west beyond the Pillars of Hercules and the Straits of Gibraltar is recorded in Plato's *Timaeus* and *Critias*. It appears to have come originally from Egypt and the source of the tale is attributed by some to a volcanic eruption on the Aegean island of Santorini, around 1450 BC. In an isolated Atlantic island community, such a story can easily be adapted to suit the locality, particularly when folklore contains a giant named Atla. Mrs Thompson was the sole teacher at Sandness Primary School from the early 1950s till her retirement. In my time there, the school roll averaged about eight. Her motivational methods (that is the kindest term) set a high proportion of graduates on their way, but she would not suffer fools in any temper. The school itself was a model of its kind when built in the late 19th century. It was due to the vision and persistence of the then head-teacher Robert Jamieson (no relation), who raised the funds by public subscription. Of his own four children, two became professors and his daughter Christina Jamieson (also my mother's married name) emerged as a well-loved local poet and folklorist.

ATLANTIS

Missis Tomsin telt dim
a'da sungkin laand
'at slippit inanundir

wast an fram fæ
Afriek's mukkil hill,
quhar Atlas stød himsel,

hunghsin up da globb
læk'it wis choost a stobb
he's kerrjin fæ da banghs –

an foo Sjætlin's singkin
sloalie still, choost da taps
a'antiek mowntins

at rekt fæ Nevis nort
an æst tæ Jotunhiemen,
noo Atlantik diep an lost.

Apo da bakk o a shiet
left owir fæ pæprin butt,
he took his pen an droo

da ootlyn o an ylind,
a laand læk Yrlind,
grien an boannie,

an he krissint'it 'Atlantis',
in onnir a'da chyint,
his æin lost laand.

An he næmt da hills an loghs,
he næmt da toons an broghs
an gied'it oardir.

A laand wie waatir fir a boardir,
læk Sjætlin, sookit inanundir,
Atlantik diep an lost.

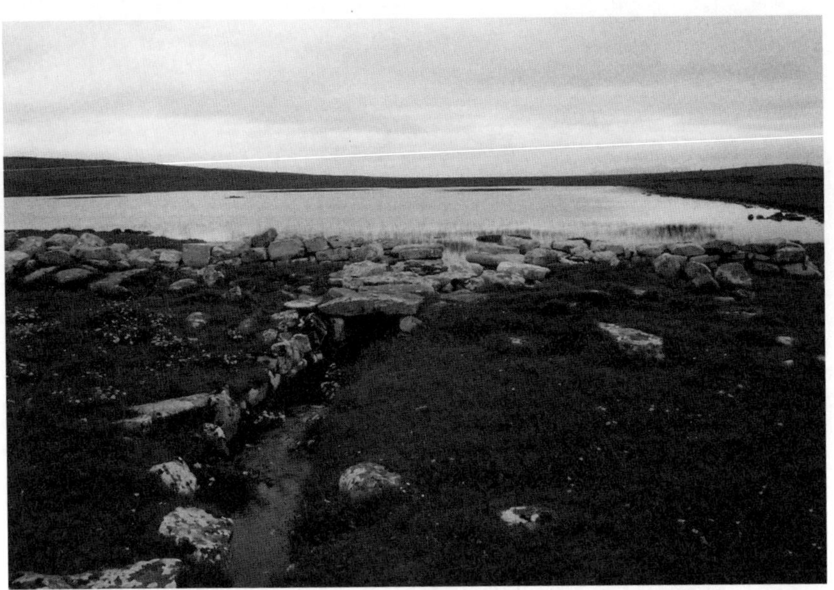

Mrs Thompson told them of the sunken land that slipped beneath

west and far from Africa's great hill, where Atlas himself stood,

holding up the globe as if it was a lump of driftwood he was carrying
    from the shore –

and that Shetland was sinking slowly still, just the tops of ancient
    mountains

that had reached from Nevis north and east to Jotunheimen, now
    Atlantic deep and lost.

On the back of a sheet left over from papering the kitchen, he took
    his pen and drew

the outline of an island, a land like Ireland, green and beautiful,

And christened it 'Atlantis', in honour of the giant, his own lost land.

And he named the hills and lakes, he named the towns and castles, and
    gave it order.

A land with water for a border, like Shetland, sucked in and under,
    Atlantic deep and lost.

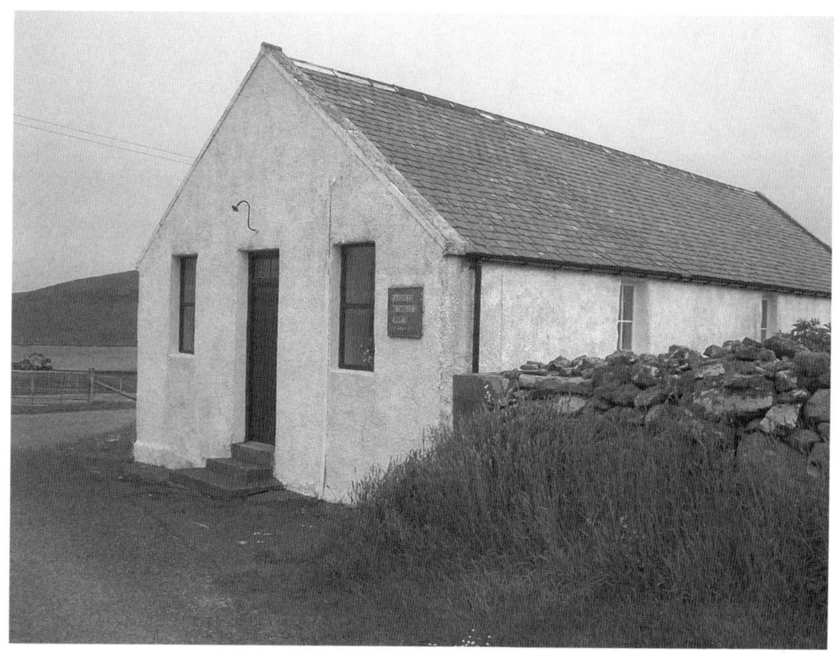

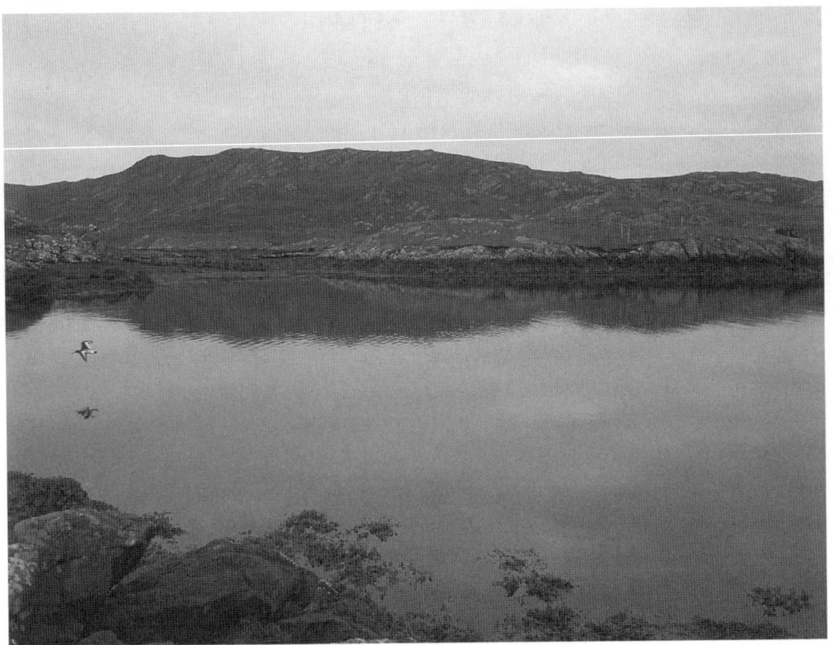

METHODIST METAPHOR

Methodism became popular in Shetland during the 19th century, when evangelising missions swept over the islands, saving souls and preaching temperance. Through this conduit, a more colourful English model crept into the islands' religious habits, more joyous than the established Church of Scotland with its emphasis on Calvinist theology, and socially much less dictatorial than the extreme forms of Protestantism in other sea-faring parts of Scotland. The importance of religious belief in communities where loss at sea is a regular fact of existence is no less prominent today. This poem represents a kind of coming into awareness of language and the variance between the local tongue and the English of the chapel.

METADIST METAFIR

Ati'da plen widdin chappil
at da Noarbie koarnir,
ati'da pierie Metadist kirk,

he likks an stikks
da mukkil kullirt stamps
a'Chiesis an'is mieriekils.

Jun en a'Him ati'da bow a'da boat
on Galilie – 'Pæs be still.'
An him choost waakin owir da shien!

He tinks – Quhitna kynd a'krættir
kood waak apo da waatir,
kood pæsiefy da storm?

Oh, holie holie holie,
sjörlie Gød's æin bærn,
næ iddir en ava.

He sings – 'An I will makk ju
fyshirs a'men, fyshirs a'men,
fyshirs a'men.'

An tinks – Quhitna mesh a'net
wid du nied fir a shaal a'men?
Ir wid du choost harpoon dim?

Na, hit's aniddir kjettil d'ir kaatchin,
hit's jun iddir wy a'spækin
Mestir Milin kaas 'metafir'.

Hit mann bie a tekkil
fir a metad-fyshin.

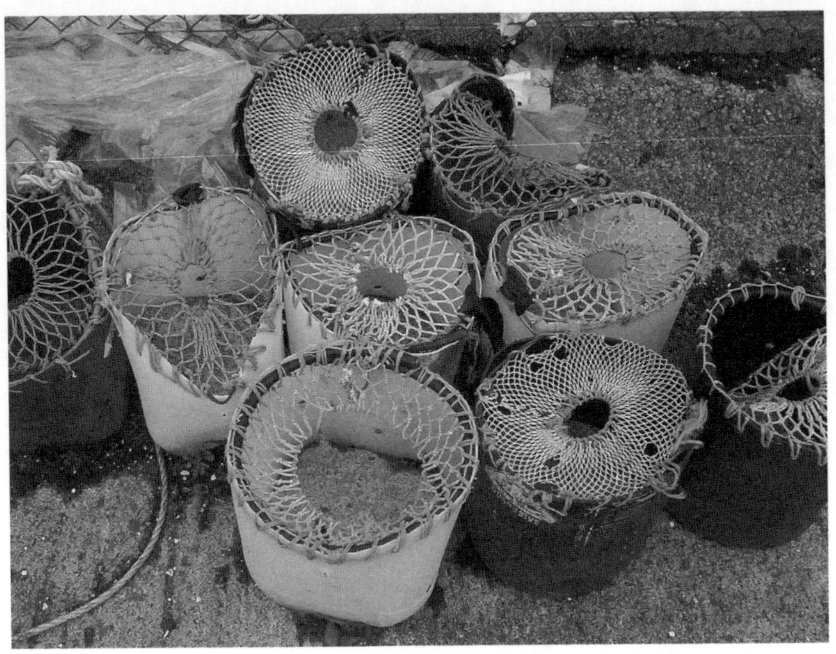

In the plain wooden chapel, at the Norby corner, in the small
Methodist church,

he licks and sticks the large coloured stamps of Jesus and his
miracles.

That picture of Him in the bow of the boat on Galilee,– 'Peace, be still.'
And Him just walking over the surface of the water!

He thinks – What kind of creature could walk on water, could calm
the storm?

O, holy, holy, holy, surely God's own child, no other.

He sings – 'And I will make ye fishers of men, fishers of men, fishers
of men.'

And thinks – What size of net would you need for a shoal of men? Or
would you just harpoon them?

No, it's another kettle they're catching, it's that other way of
speaking Mister Milne calls 'metaphor'.

It must be the tackle for method-fishing.

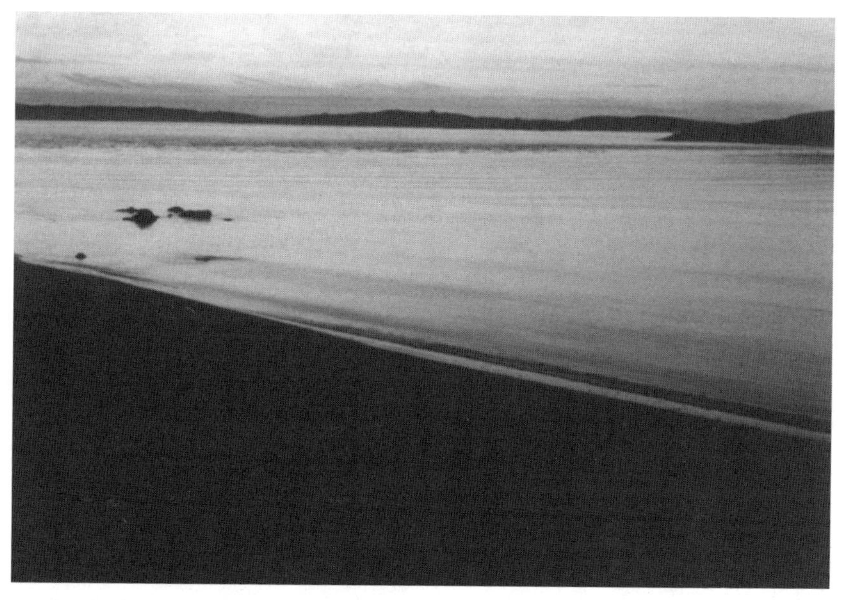

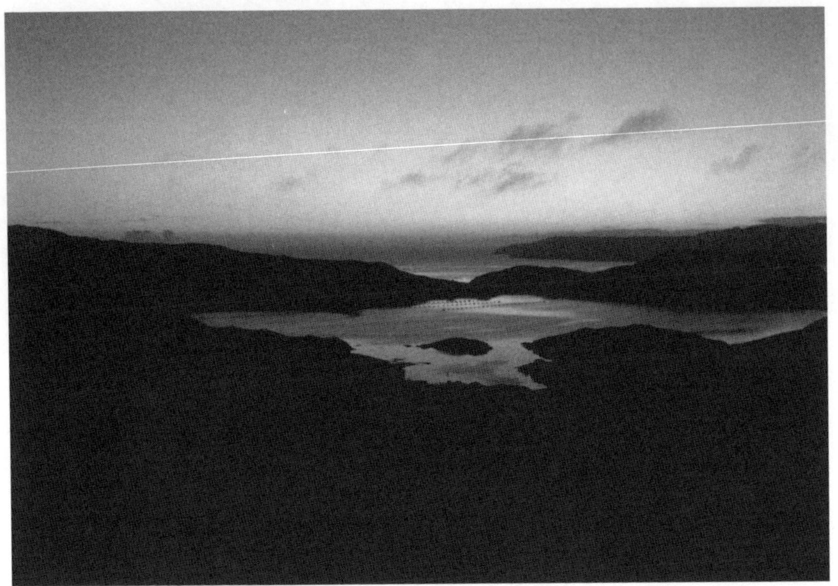

CONSTANT STAR

In the land of 'summer dim', night is a brief darkening, even as dawn is shining above the northern horizon. In winter, darkness invades and tyrannises the day. The lighthouse at Eshaness was a constant in these changing skies, bright summer and dark winter alike, both signalling and receiving: the lamp, a beacon, twinkling; while the keeper's eye scanned the sea, like 'Da Gødman' – a local term for Jesus, 'the good shepherd'. Now unmanned, its function is only that of star, signalling. The lighthouse no longer sees.

KONSTINT STARN

Simmirdim kam doon aboot da Niep
an up abøn da krug a'Æshnis,
lyght læ owir da nortlaand læk a hap.

Æ solitrie ee's ay blinkrin,
choost is it dös a'da blakk hert a'wintir.
Aa aroond swalls up an dwyns,

grows up grien, dan widdirs awa –
mønrys an sunfaa,
niep tyd an voar tyd.

Konstelæsjin's drap ablo da laand
an iddirs rys t'kut a njoo shæp
ati'da chænchin hievins,

bit Æshnis lyght's ay blinkrin –
blink, blink, blinkrin – a starn ee
waatchin, waatchin an shynin.

He tinks – Hit's gød t'ken
Da Gødman's dær.

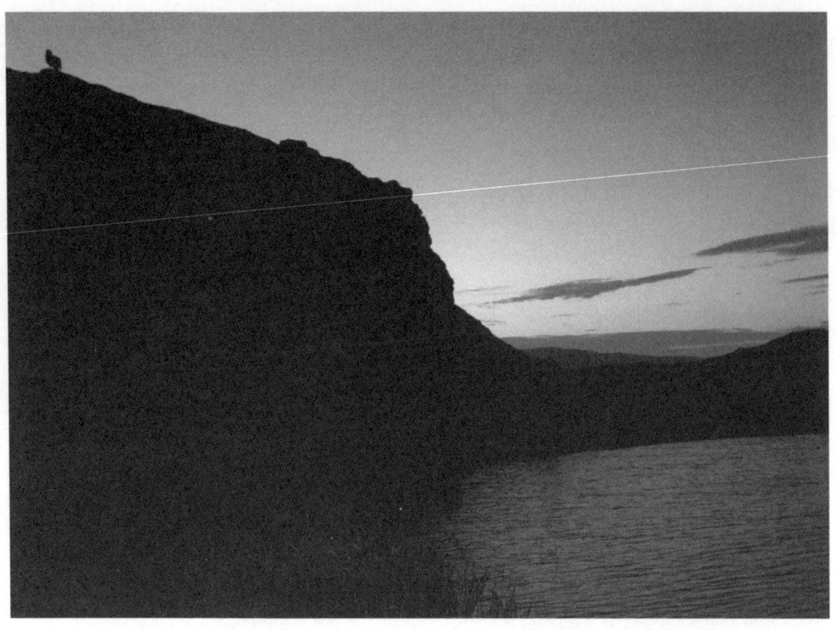

Summer's dim came down about the cliffs, and up above the crouching
  body of Eshaness, light lay over the northland like a shawl.

One solitary eye keeps blinking, just as it does in the black heart of
  winter. All around swells up and dwindles,

grows up green, then withers away – Moonrise and sunset, neap tide
  and spring tide.

Constellations drop below the land and others rise to cut a new shape
  in the changing heavens,

but Eshaness light's always blinking – blink, blink, blinking – a star
  eye watching, watching and shining.

He thinks – It's good to know the Shepherd's there.

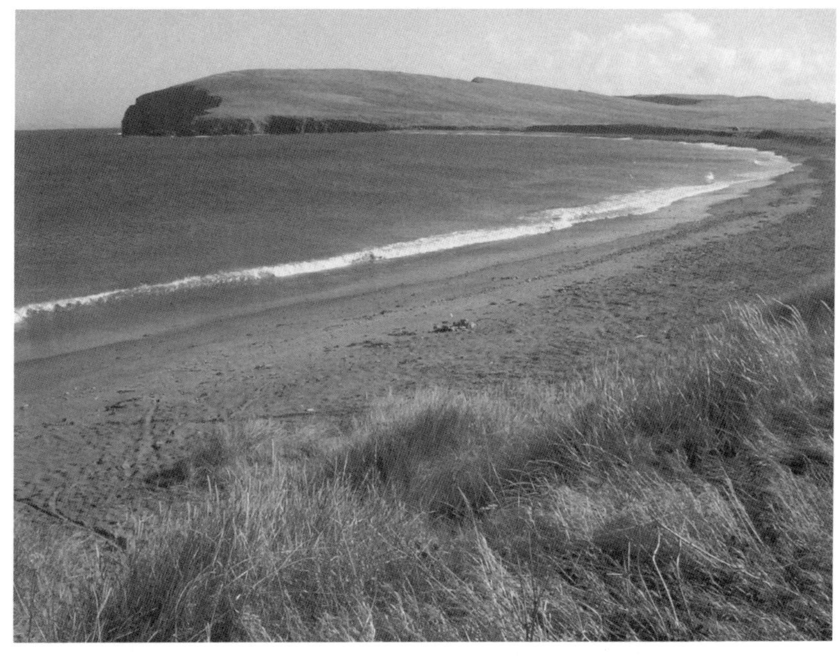

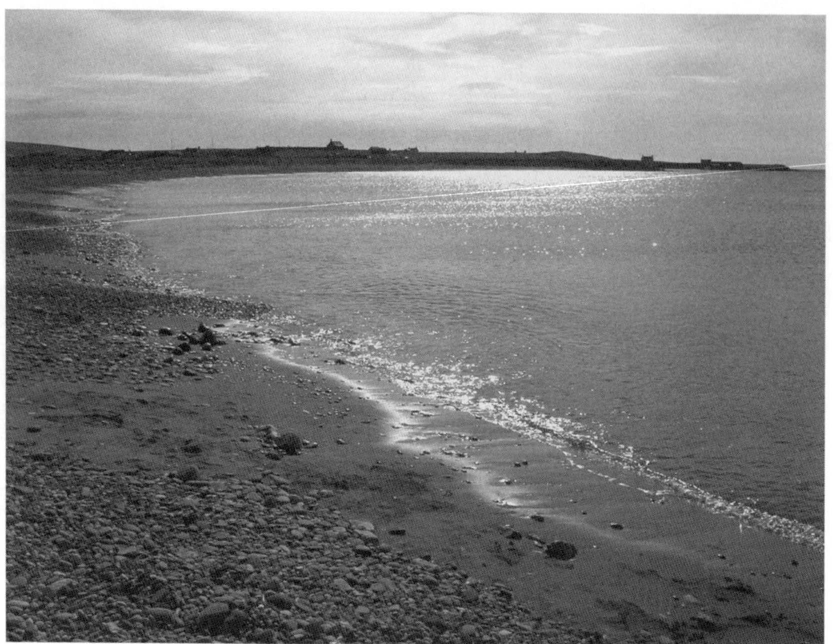

BOTTLED

Hay's of Aberdeen, makers and purveyors of soft drinks, were famed throughout the north of Scotland. Their sweet cordial concentrates, drunk neat despite the 'dilute to taste' instruction, were regarded as a winter treat, given to children in spirit glasses with sweet biscuits when they went out 'guizing' round the houses at the festivals of Halloween, Christmas Eve or Hogmanay. The 'message in the bottle' of this poem did find a beachcomber's hand elsewhere, but rather than the foreign shores of Iceland, Norway, Faroe or Denmark, it reached no further than the 'northland' on the other side of St Magnus Bay.

BOTTILT

Hit wis a Hæie's chinchir koardjil
he baalt owir da fæs a'da wæjiev
wie his haandskrivin 'po da pæpir insyd.

Da Hæie's korks snødit tyghtir,
wid kiep his ingkie messiech
dry fir da wirld t'fin.

Fæ dis laandfaa, he myght rekk
oot ta Riekjaviek ir Tromsø,
t'Heligolaand ir Tor's Havn.

He nivir dootit an ungkin haand
wid lift Hæie's bottil
fæ an ebbin grund sumwy.

Dan dir kam a lettir bakk. A man'd fun it,
ati'da shoormil, an wret, wie fotoos,
fæ dat ungkin laand akross da sie –

Æshnis.

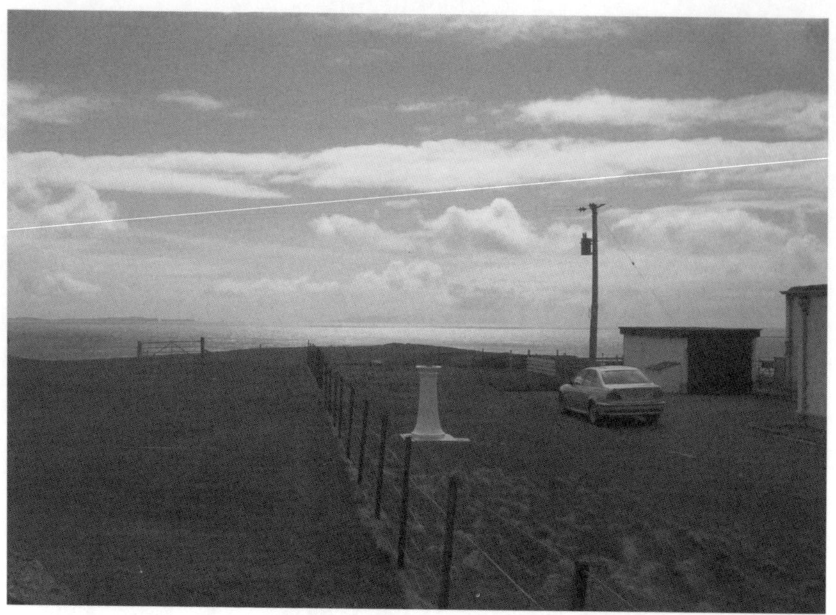

It was a Hay's ginger cordial bottle he threw beyond the incoming
wave, with his handwriting on the paper inside.

Hay's corks twisted tighter, would keep his inky message dry for the
world to read.

From this shore, he might reach out to Rekjavik or Tromsø, to
Heligoland or Torshavn.

He never doubted a stranger's hand would pick Hay's bottle from an
ebbing shoreline somewhere.

Then a letter came. A man had found it, in the shallows, and wrote,
with photos, from that foreign land across the sea –

Eshaness.

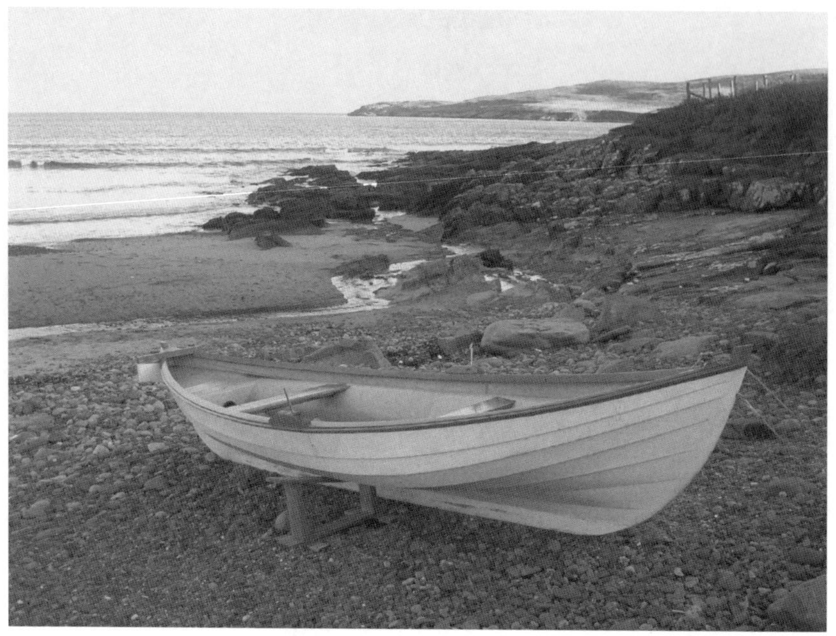

AT THE EELA

'Da Eela' is the inshore summer fishing, which once supplied many a winter meal with salted fish. Originally the term referred to the habit of anchoring the boat at tried and tested spots. The word 'eela' is reckoned to derive from the Old Norse 'ili', meaning a stone with a rope fastened to it, serving as a rudimentary anchor.

AT DA EELA

Æ fyn nyght
lyn fyshin
wie sum a'da aald men,

lissnin t'stoaries
as sjærp as da sie-ær,
a hjook slips his grip,

kuts trow wiet skiejin,
tærs his toom opin
an he fiels da saat byt.

Haalt fæ da depts,
piltiks sprikkil, glissin,
glæpin fir waatir,

gills flaapin, die.
Bløe fæ da hjook merk
drips ati'da oshin –

glæmin broon sie lævs a'tang
swiem firnenst da grien spaars
atill a kaald wiet wirld

as da lyns wind oot.

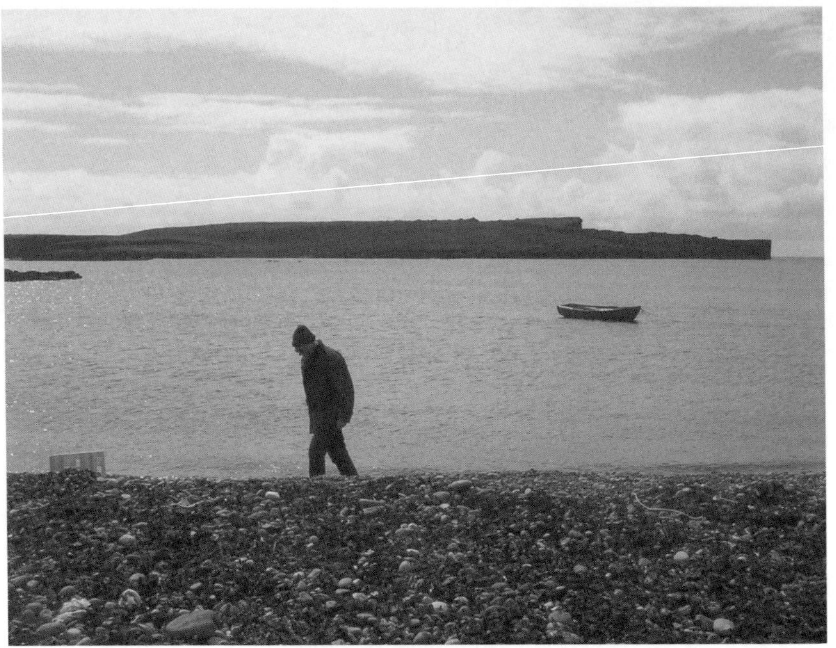

One fine night, line fishing with some of the old men,
listening to stories as sharp as the sea air, a hook slips from his grip,
cuts through wet skin, tears his thumb open, and he feels the salt bite.
Hauled from the depths, young coalfish wriggle, glisten, gulping for
    water,
gills flapping, die. Blood from the hook mark drips in the ocean –
gleaming brown sea leaves of weed swim beneath the green spars in
    a cold wet world
as the lines wind out.

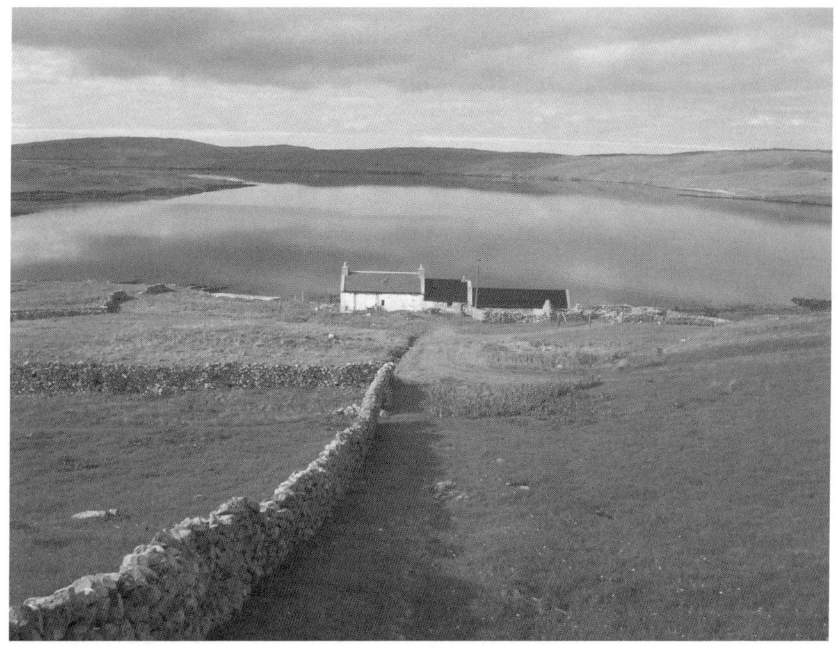

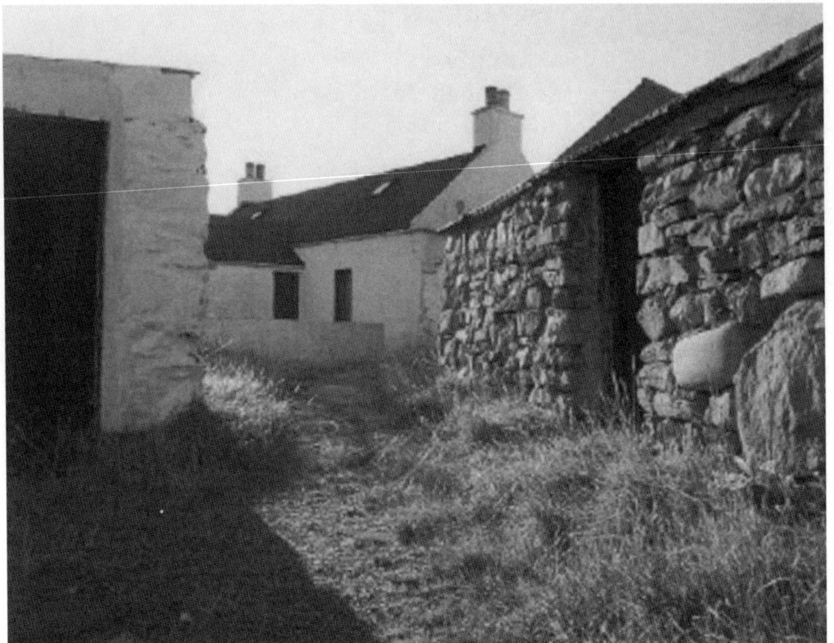

BOTABIT

This is the division of the catch between those who had shared in the fishing, including a portion to the elderly or infirm of the village. The custom's name derives from the Old Norse 'bata-byti', the 'sharing of a boat's catch'.

But no gift was taken without some return of kindness, so in this case the gift of hot scones from the griddle had to be eaten. Sea hunger satisfied decorum.

BOTABIT

Wun ashoar,
da boat up a'da noost,
da tekkil sortit,

da katsh's mæsjirt oot
in bukkits, dievydit
up atwien da hoosis.

Da pyps ir oot,
da riek kloods roond,
da njoosin lingirs ati'da hömin.

'Ja,'
he'll tak twaartrie dær –
ta Miena's poarch doar.

'Hieir,'
prood a'da pukkil gien
t'dem'at hedna mukkil.

Shö takks da pæl-foo fæ'im
an shö bids'im 'Kum de wis,'
an shö makks'im sit

an staps'im bannik-foo.

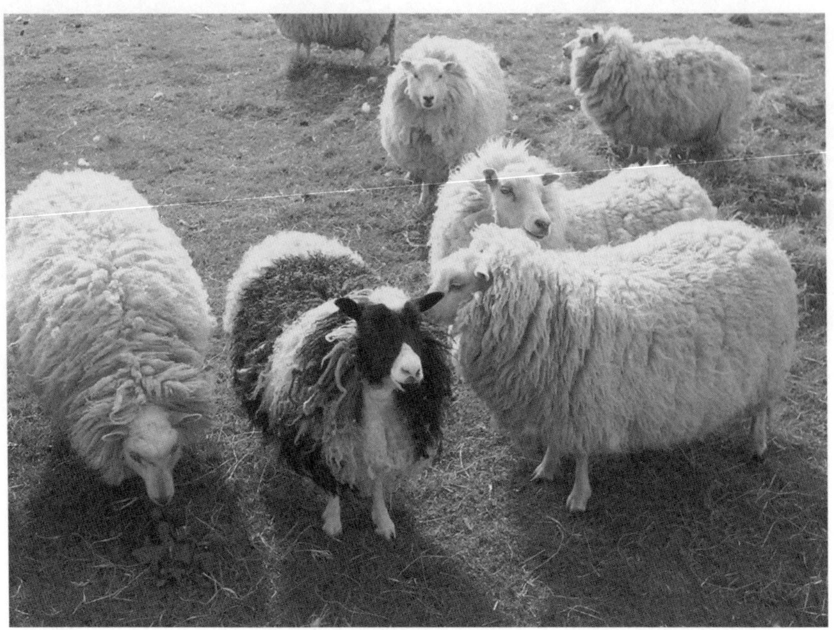

Once ashore, the boat up in its resting place, the tackle sorted,

the catch is measured out in buckets, divided between houses.

The pipes are out, the smoke clouds round, the conversation lingers
in the summer twilight.

'Yes,' he'll take a few fish there – to Mina's porch door.

'Here,' proud of the portion given to those who haven't much.

She takes the full bucket from him, and bids him 'come inside,' and
she makes him sit,

and fills him full of bannocks.

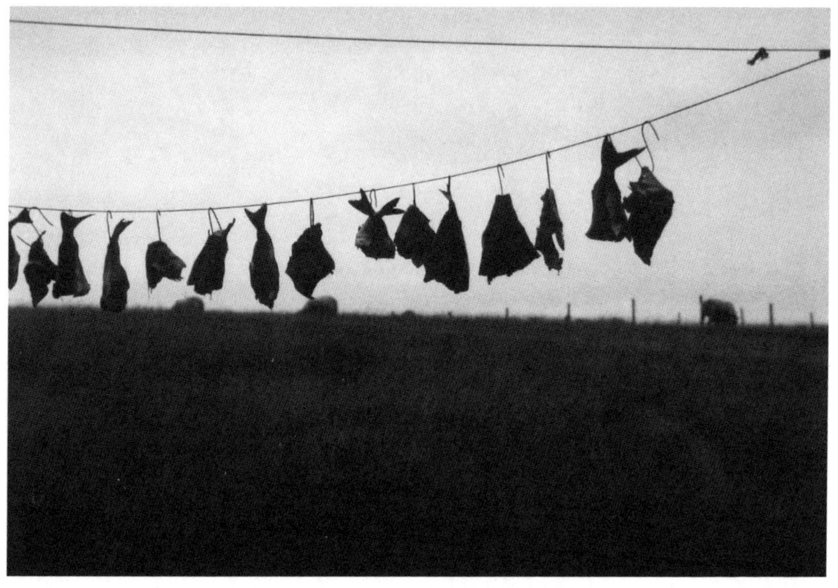

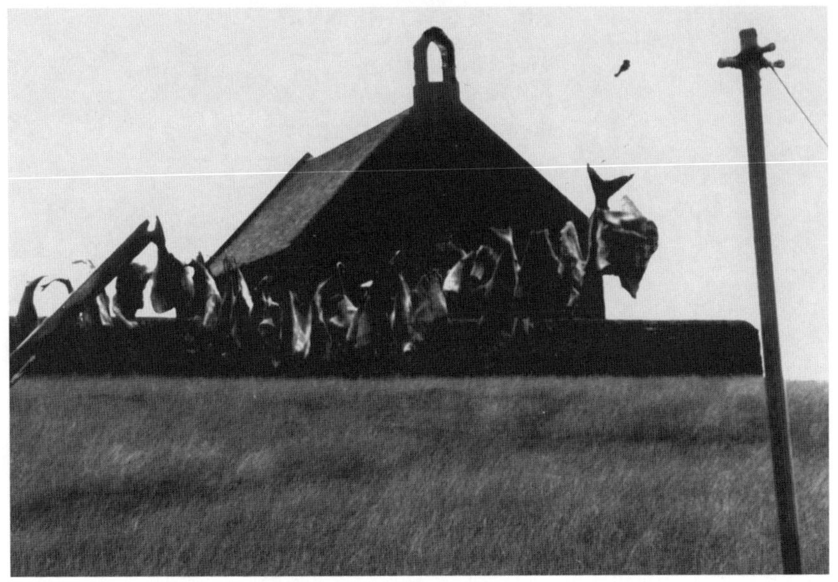

COARSE SALT AND SNOW

Once gutted and cleaned, the fish that could not be eaten at the time were salted by immersion in a barrel of pickle. After the allotted period, the fish were hung to dry outside – and later, brought inside, near to the peat fire. The means of discovering when the coarse salt and water mixture was the right consistency involved placing an onion or a potato in the barrel – if it floated, the mixture was salty enough.

KOORS SAAT AN SNAA

Twa days eftir
he waaks amung
da waashin lyns a'dryin fysh

hingin ootsyd hoosis
læk kut-oot strings
a'choynt-up men

da bærns makk
wie fowldit pæpir
an a pær a'sjiers.

Siks munt lætir,
ati'da hert a'Jøl,
wie da snaa apo da ært

da unjin ati'da pikkil drum
willa med da maachikk happin
an a saat tung'll mynd apo

dat lang simmir nyght
da katsh wis tæn.

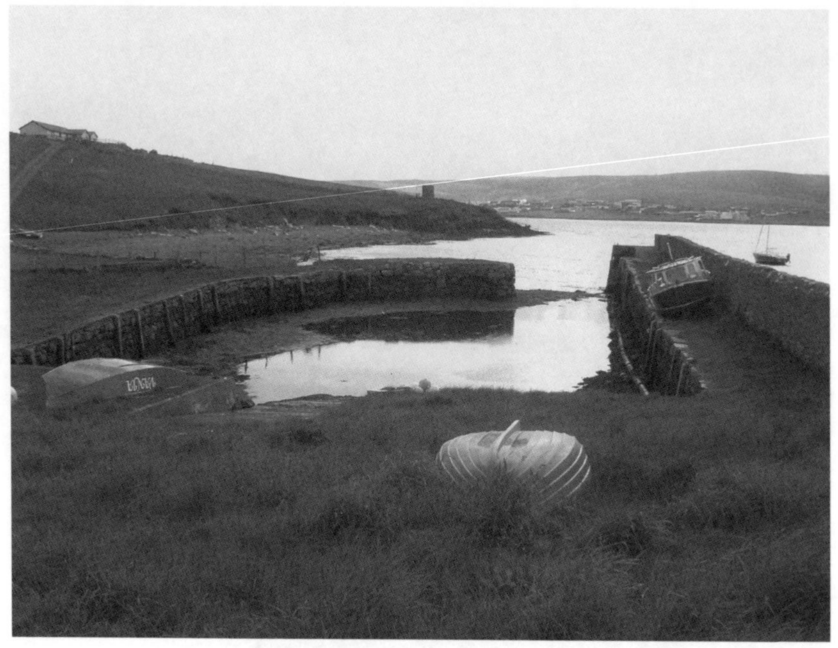

Two days later, he walks among the washing lines of drying fish
hanging outside houses, like cut-out strings of joined-up men
the children make with folded paper and a pair of scissors.
Six months later, in the heart of the Christmas holidays, when the
    snow's upon the ground,
the onion in the pickle drum will have made the magic happen and a
    salty tongue will then remember
the long summer night when the catch was taken.

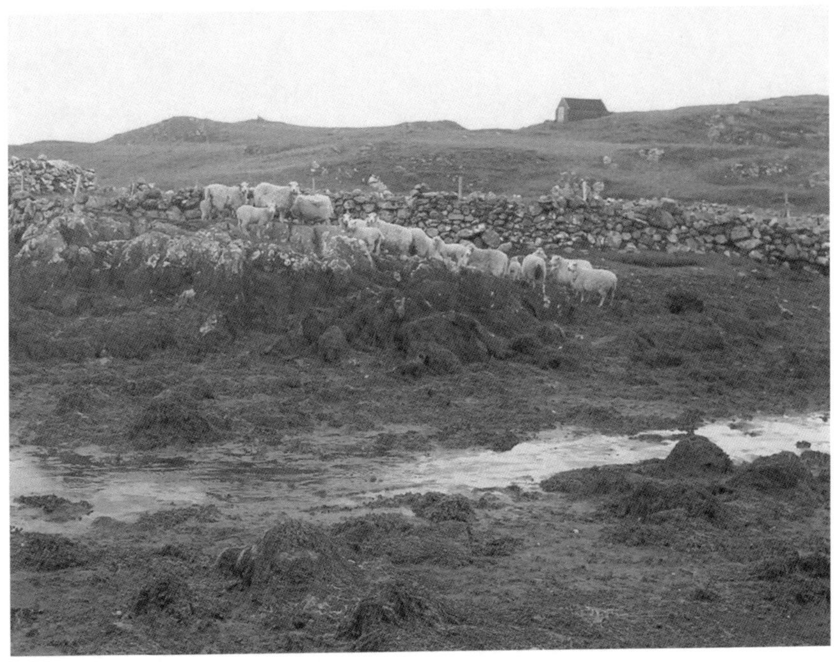

II
ANTIEK SIE MEN

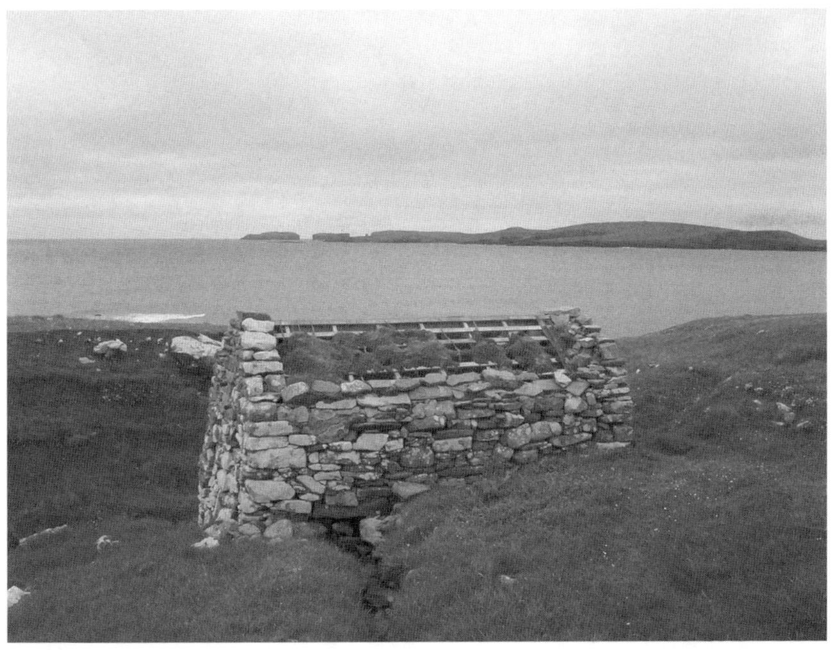

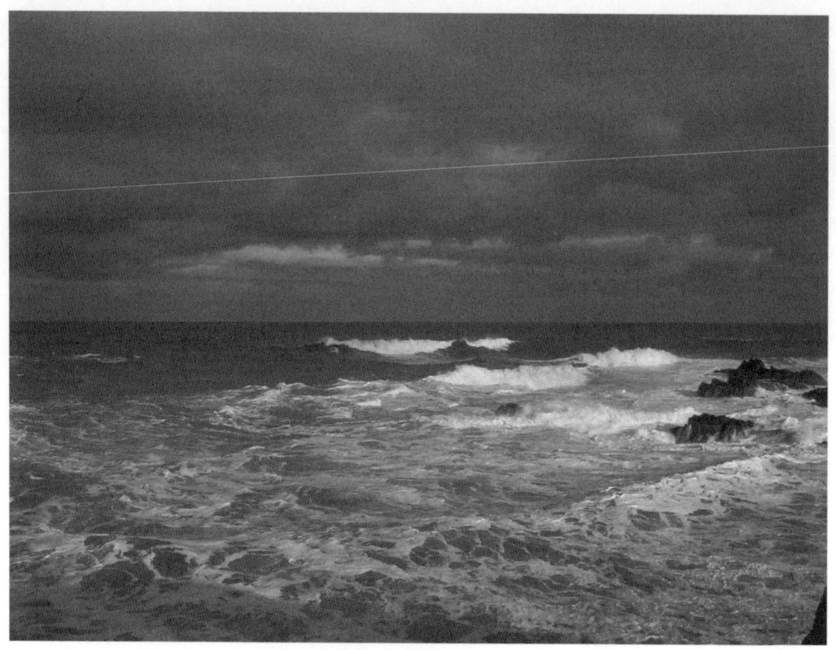

LAMENT FOR THE THIRSTY

The westside of Shetland has been 'dry' through most of the last century, having been particularly influenced by the Temperance movement – not that this prevented the dedicated from drinking. But it did mean that those who wanted a bottle would have to arrange circuitous methods to obtain it, perhaps sending to Lerwick for a brown-paper-wrapped package on the bus – or as one man habitually did, undertaking what was sometimes a hazardous journey, across the bay to Hillswick. There the oldest pub in Shetland, 'Da Bød', might satisfy thirst.

LAAMINT FIR DA TRISTIE

Kooshin Bill wis lost
heddit fir Hillswiek
akross Sænt Magnis Bæ

on a koors nyght
in an opin boat –
fokk sed

he wis gjaain
t'da bød dær –
(fir drink!)

He tinks – Aa dat waatir!
Man, hit's dry t'die a'drooth
amung sæ mukkil waatir.

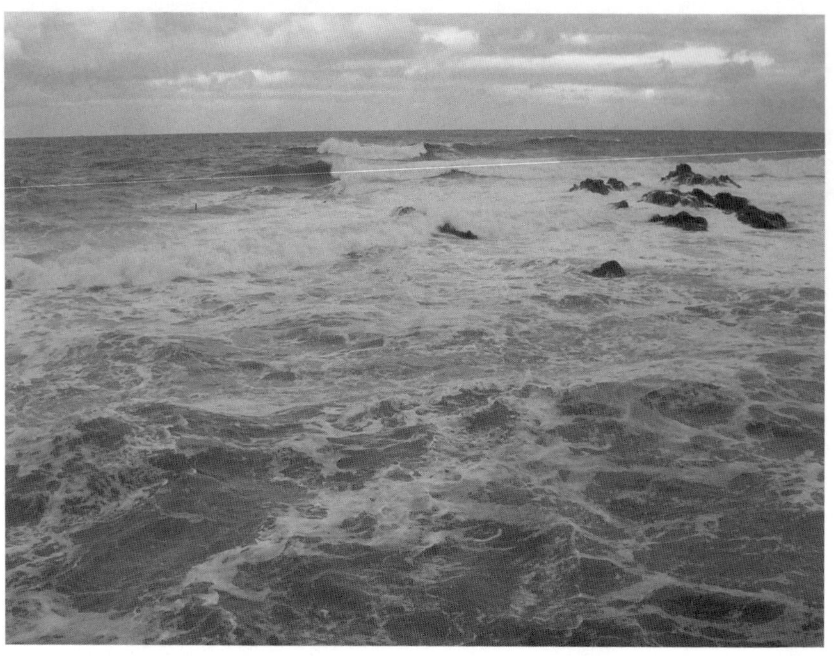

Cousin Bill was drowned, heading for Hillswick across St Magnus Bay
on a stormy night in an open boat – People said
he was going to the pub there – (for drink!)
He thinks – All that water! Man, it's ironic to die of thirst in the midst
    of so much water.

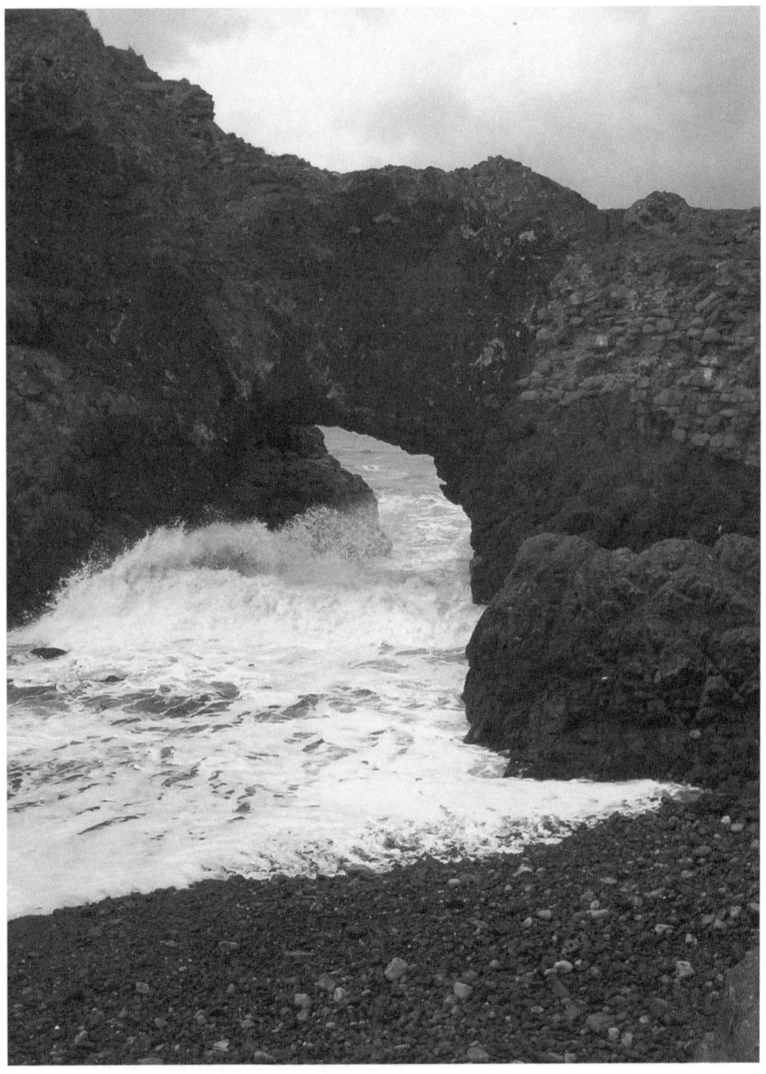

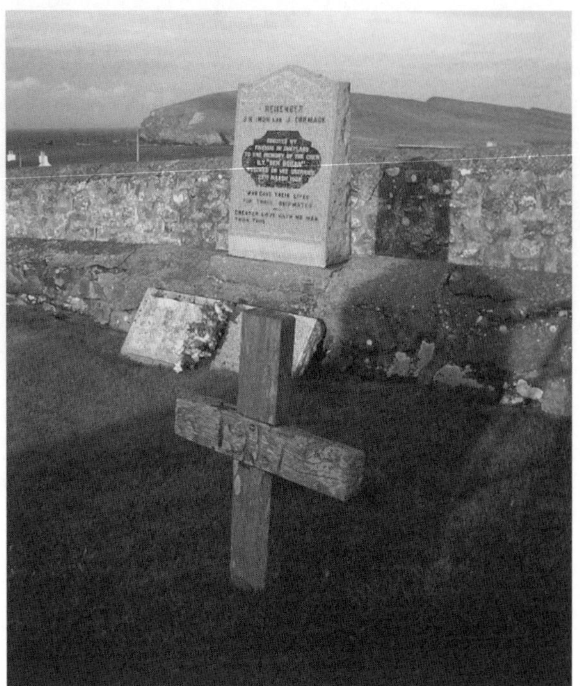

SHARK'S TEETH

The *Ben Doran* was one of the most tragic of shipwrecks. Although the would-be rescuers were able to reach the stranded vessel in time, they were unable to save the men because of the ferocity of the storm. The Ve Skerries are infamous as 'a graveyard of ships', and lie to the north-west of Sandness and Papa Stour. Folklore has it that they were boulders thrown by the giant, Atla, when he sat in the middle of the mainland hills at Weisdale, amusing himself – a less helpful giant than his near name-sake, the classical Atlas. The name comes from Old Norse: some say from 'va', meaning 'danger', others that it is a contraction of 'vestan' or 'western'. The individual skerries are North Skerry, Ormal, The Clubb, Reaverack, and Helligobolo. A lighthouse was built there in 1979, following the wrecking of the trawler *Elinor Viking*.

HO'S BYTIRS

Aa da men wir lost
quhan da *Ben Doran* ran
apo da Ve Skerries.

Aa lost in 1930.
An still da rieth kam ivrie jieir
fae da wyf'at grannie wrot ta.

He sies da Ve Skerries
rys læk da fins a'da serpint
oot a'dat grævjæird, Atla's sie –

an emtie græjievs ir markit
bie shærp shærk's bytirs
ati'da kirkjærd, noo.

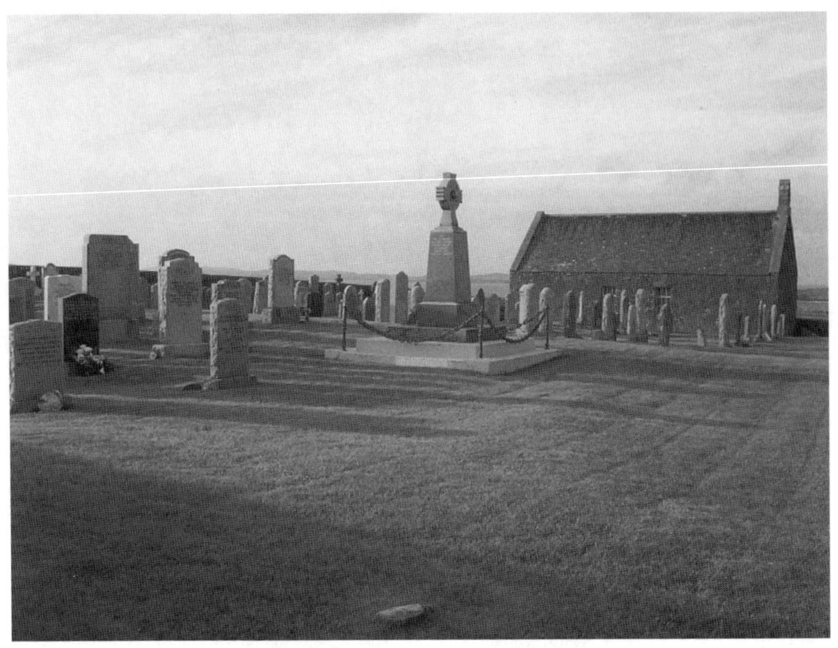

All the men were lost when the *Ben Doran* wrecked upon the danger skerries.

All were lost in 1930. And still the wreath came every year, from the widow his grandmother wrote to.

He sees the danger skerries rise like the fins of the serpent, out of that graveyard, Atla's sea –

And empty graves are marked by sharp sharks' teeth in the churchyard, now.

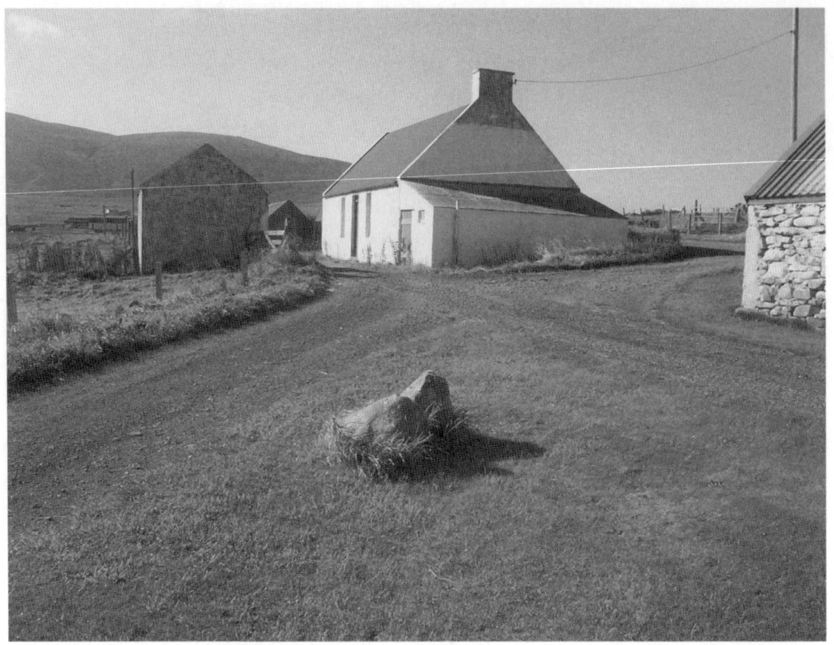

PAPA BOAT

The ferry from the island of Papa Stour, the 'big island of the Holy Fathers' of the Celtic church and an important centre in Norse times, came to Sandness across the Atlantic current that swept through the channel between the two. Until, that is, in an effort to better shelter the exposed pier, the council dumped large quantities of stone on its seaward side, with the result that the pier silted up. The 'Papa Boat' now operates from West Burrafirth, a few miles along the coast, travelling with the tidal stream, rather than across it. Papa is famous locally as the place where the 'Hippies' first arrived in the early 70s, after a local man had placed an advert in one of the Sunday papers seeking settlers to turn the tide of depopulation. 'Stour' derives from the Old Norse 'stør', meaning 'great' or 'large', and contrasts with the nearby, but now uninhabited, Papa Little.

PAPA BOAT

Ungkin Papa men
kam owir t'Melbie pieir,
kam trekksin up da lang kirk bræ,

trællin mukkil ojil drums,
fyv-gallin-full fir fjooil,
t'da Saanis shop.

Da purlin a'da petril
as'it faas fæ d'aald bress tap
in ati'da drum-mooth's

laek da purrin a'da poorie,
an mynds'im a'his middir's
tendir med-up krib-sang –

'Row, pierie bojies,
akross da sie,
ju'll sjøn bie in Papa.'

He tinks – Ja, bit still
dat kat kan kloor, an Papa
Soond's a færs tyd-ræs

a'wyld Atlantik waatir
'at monie-a-dæ ati'wintir
næ Papa boat'll kross,

fir aa dæ hæ dir petril,
dir enchins foo a'fjooil,
at hem on Papa Stooir.

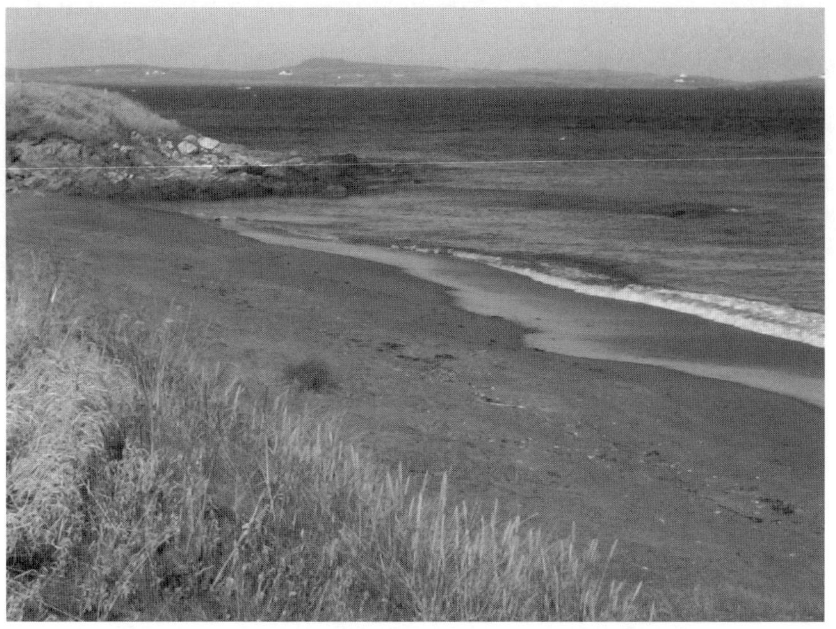

The strange men of Papa came over to the Melby pier, trudging up the
    long slope to the church,

carrying their big five gallon drums for fuel, to the Sandness shop.

The sound of the petrol as it falls from the old brass tap, into the
    open mouth of the drum is

like the purring of the cat, and reminds him of his mother's tender
    made-up lullaby –

'Row, little boys, across the sea, you'll soon be in Papa.'

He thinks – Yes, but still that cat can scratch, and Papa Sound's so
    fierce a tidal race

of wild Atlantic water that often in the winter no Papa ferry will cross,

for all they have their petrol, their engines full of fuel, at home on
    Papa Stour.

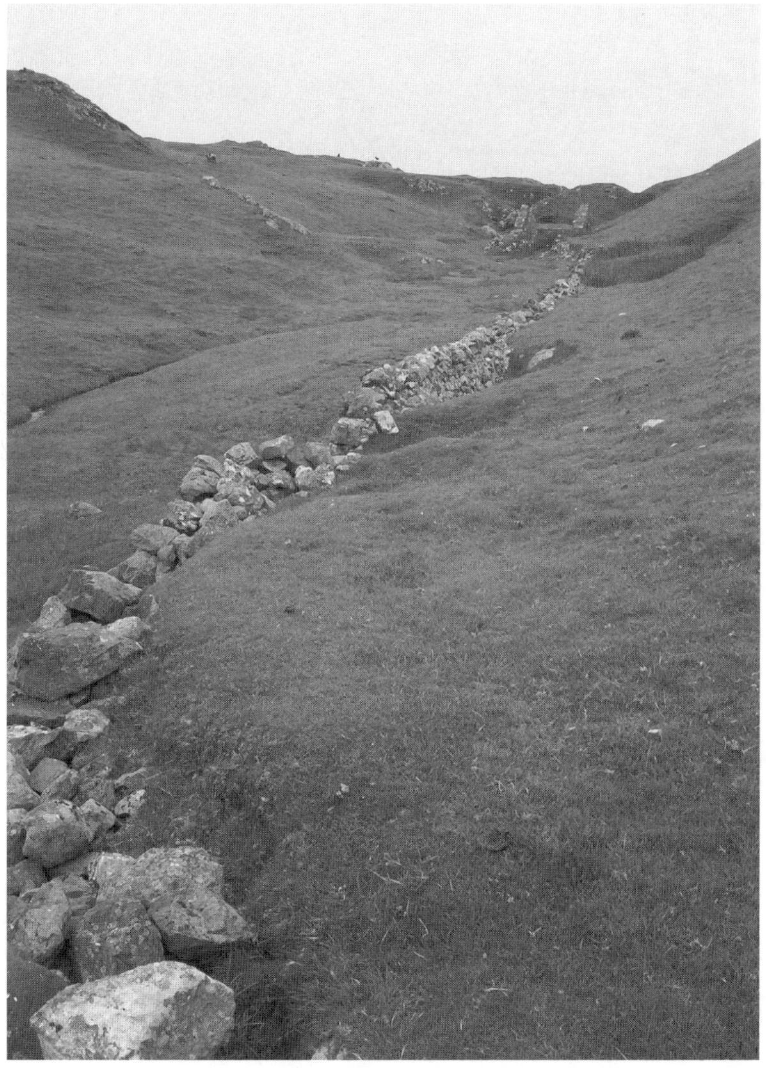

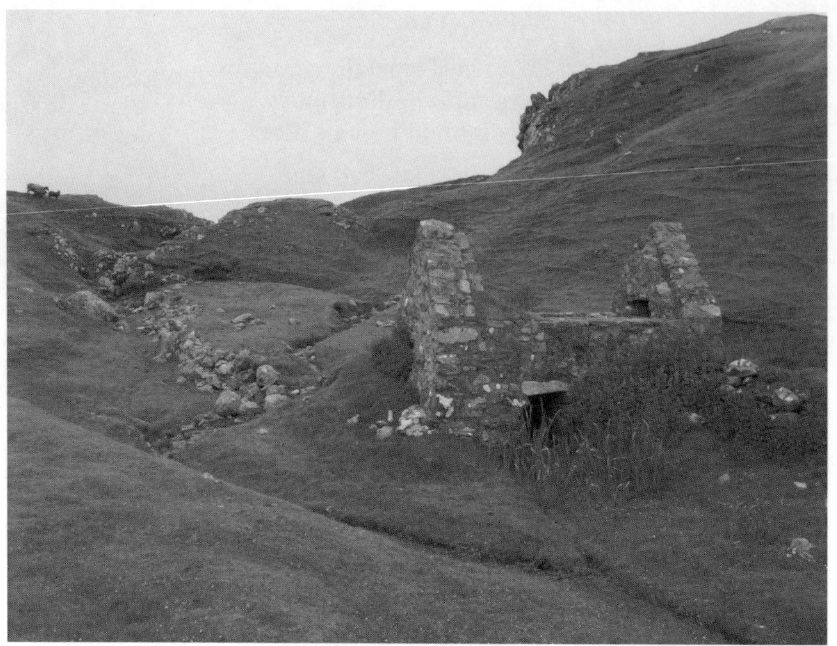

PAPA LITTLE

A small island at the heart of a system of sea lochs to the landward of St Magnus Bay, near Gonfirth, Papa Little is where my maternal line originated – the only family to occupy this island in recent times, although its name suggests that it was once home to the wandering Culdees of the Celtic church. The solitary house was latterly used as a summer residence for a shepherd. After the peat supply ran out on Papa Stour, islanders would travel by boat to the smaller namesake, and ferry their fuel supply home. The poem recalls a rare family reunion, when four siblings gathered with their children to visit the island.

PAPA LITTIL

Dæ aa gied tagiddir,
trie sistirs wie dir fæmlies,
apo dir briddir Alan's boat.

Dæsie hem fæ Sheffielt,
Tissie kum fæ Saanis
an Winnie oot fæ Lerook,

t'quhaar da foarbærs kam fæ –
Papa Littil, pierie ylind a'da munks,
laangsyn diesertit.

Choost a hoos an twaartrie rigs
an haafwy up da hill
a pierie rummilt mæl-mill.

Æ fæmlie's ylind
shaltirt an boannie,
wie plentie a'pætmør.

Fæ da tap a'da Papa Littil hill
he sies, myls t'da wastirt,
da mukkil ylind a'da munks,

quhar dæ hed næ mær pæt,
an quhar dæ hed t'sæl fæ,
t'wirk da unklæmt mør

'po Papa Littil.

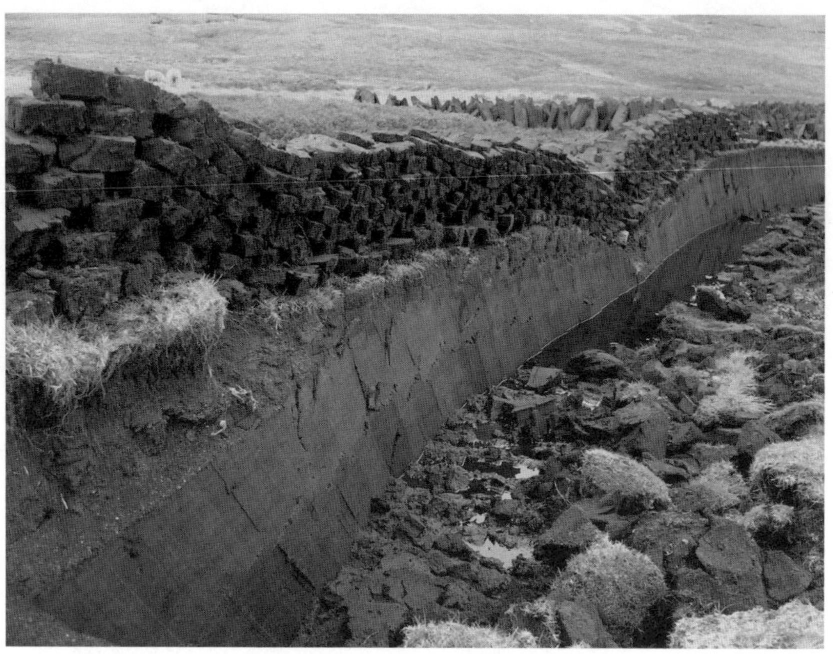

They all went together, three sisters with their families, aboard their
     brother Alan's boat.

Daisy home from Sheffield, Tissie come from Sandness, and Winnie
     out from Lerwick,

to where the forebears came from – Papa Little, smaller island of the
     monks, long since deserted.

Just one house and a few meagre fields, and halfway up the hill, a tiny
     derelict meal-mill.

One family's island, sheltered and bonny with a plentiful supply of peat.

From the top of the Papa Little hill he sees, miles to the west, the
     bigger island of the monks,

where the peat supply ran out, and where they had to sail from, to
     work the unclaimed peat-banks

on Papa Little.

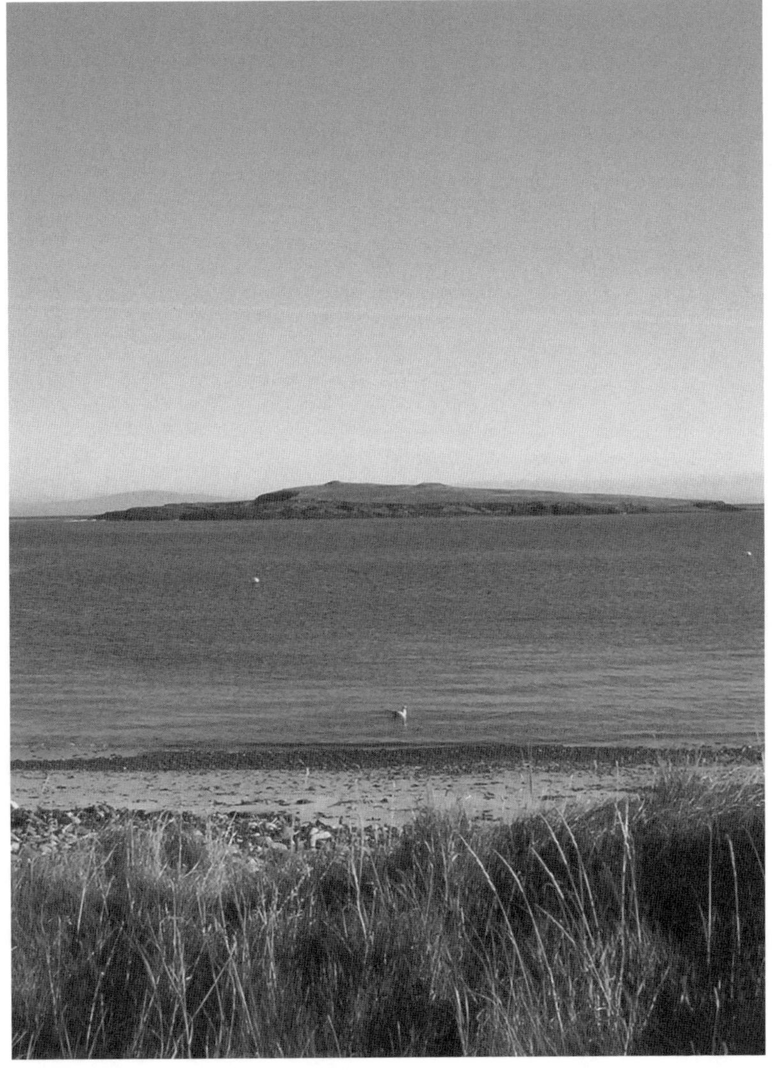

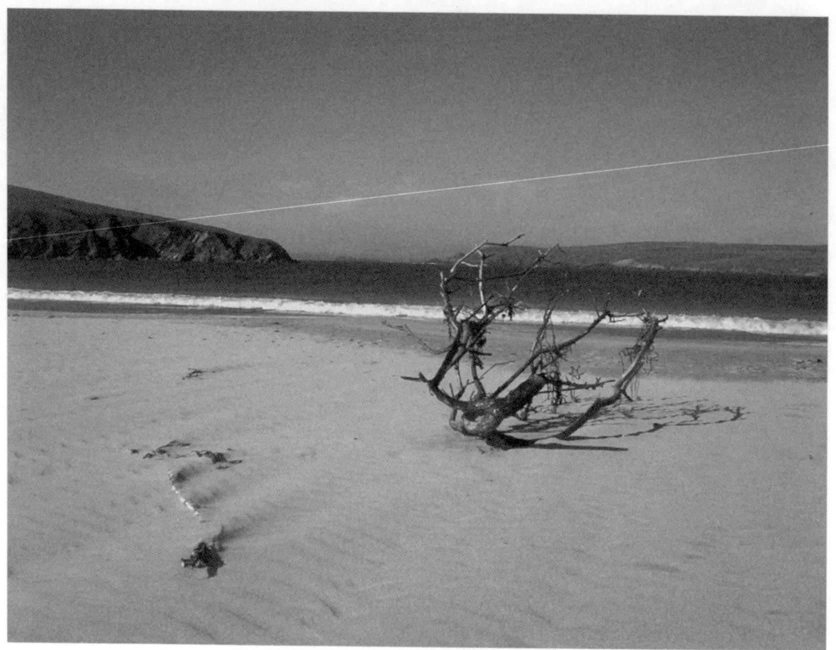

TO THE UNINHABITED ISLE

The Holm of Melby lies a few hundred metres offshore from Melby beach. A relation of mine, Peter John Pole, kept sheep there, and would make occasional trips for their maintenance. When I went there with him during lambing, I found he had hung up a dead skua as a warning to others like this pirate bird. St Ninian's Isle in the south of Shetland is similarly close to the township of Bigton, but is connected to the mainland by a sand bar, or tombolo. Here, on 4 July 1958, a schoolboy assisting on an archæological dig at the old Celtic church uncovered a valuable treasure thought to have been buried at the approach of Norse raiders. The purpose of the porpoise' bone among the silverware is uncertain. The tales of dolphins and porpoises guiding ships may be relevant. Perhaps the jawbone was a piece of sympathetic magic, intended as a symbolic guide to safety.

T'DA HUM

In a tin boie's imachinæsjin,
fattint up wie RLS,
jun pyrit tæls rin færlie wyld,

quhar da ded bungsie hings
bie a klaa, hiediekraa
apo da hyght a'da hill,

da bløda fæ da sjot in hits briest's
a waarnin t'da hoarnie nebs
dat spier a njoo-boarn lam.

Quhar atill a aald biggin,
mebbie fæ da dæs quhan Yriesh munks
upræst stæn in ootby plæsis,

he fiels an ingklin
o a bersærk's kjittil
an ettils at da livin stoarie

a'træsjir fun in fiftie-æght,
apo Sænt Ninjin's Ajil,
mann ryght enjogh bie troo.

Twintie-æght piesis a'silvir
an da chaa-bon o a niesik –
a Piktiesh troav wie a guddik kroon.

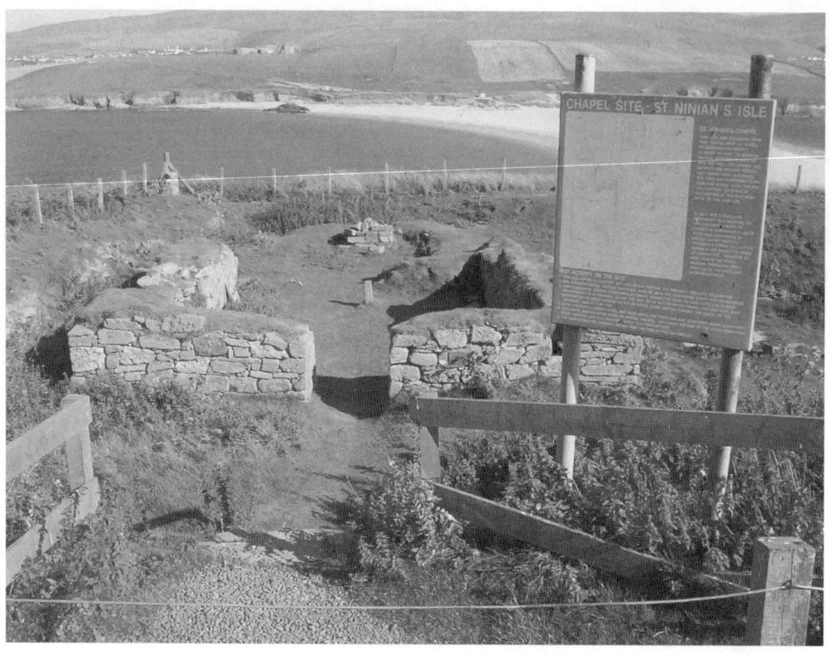

In a thin boy's imagination, fattened up with RLS, those pirate tales
    ran wild,

where the dead skua hangs by a claw, upside down on the top of the
    hill,

the blood from the shot in its breast a warning to all the horny beaks
    that seek a new-born lamb.

Here at the old steading, maybe from the days when Irish monks
    erected stones in isolated places,

he feels an inkling of a berserk's tickle and figures that the living tale

of treasure found in '58 on St Ninian's Isle, must right enough be true.

Twenty-eight pieces of silver and the jawbone of a porpoise – a Pictish
    trove with a riddle for a crown.

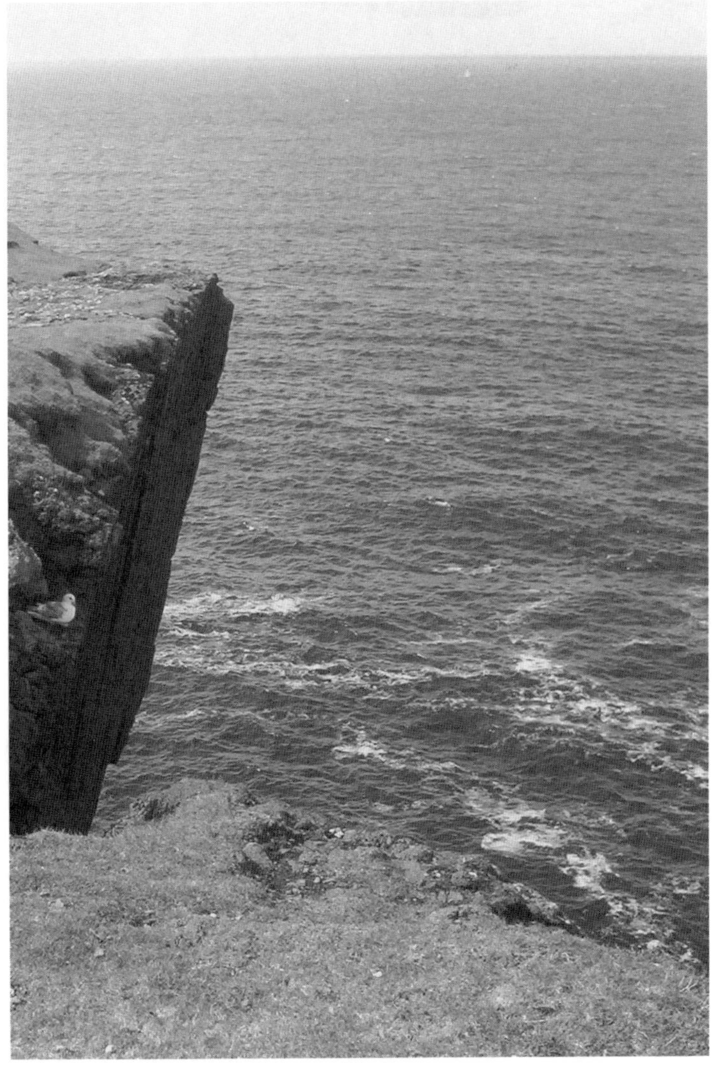

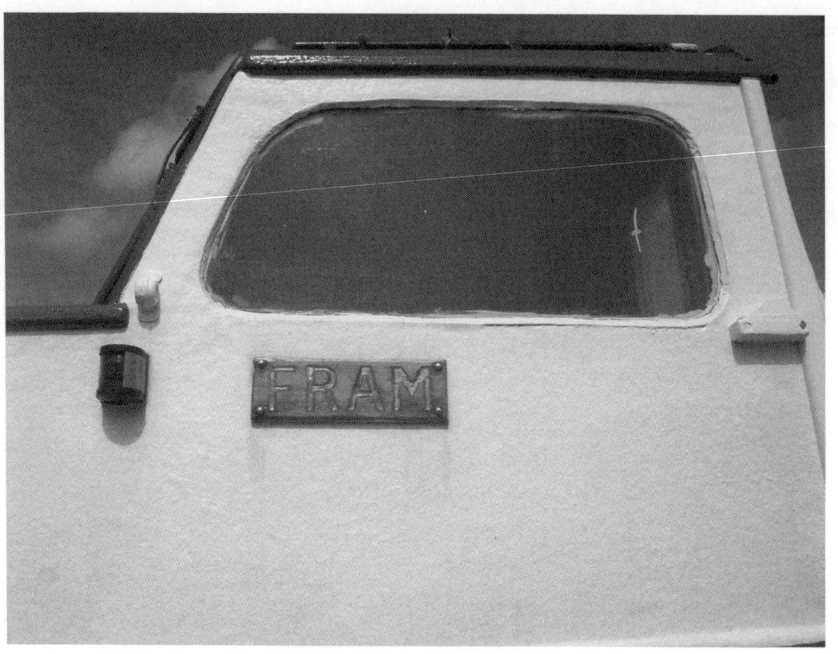

ON THE GREAT BLUE DEEP

The coming and going of sailors, home on leave and then returning to the sea, gave a regular if low frequency rhythm to life, as the higher frequency comings and goings of the ferry from Lerwick to Aberdeen, twice a week, fulfilled a similar function in punctuating island life. The word 'djoob', meaning the deep ocean beyond the continental shelf, has a pre-Teutonic root, 'dhub' and corresponds to the Old English 'deop', Old Norse 'djub', and Modern Norwegian 'dyp'.

APO DA BLOO DJOOB

T'kum bakk sæf ir no
fæ da sie broght
da wirld hem t'dim.

Da sie's da wy
da wirld kum's ta wis.
Is da boat wun in?

Nier ivrie hoos
a mærchint siemin atill'it,
fædir, ungkil, sun,

gadderin quhier pierie bits
a'da brod wirld an aa'its
fremmit tungs fir fokk t'gokk at.

Men, gien a kuppla jieir,
dat rieipier, mistierjis,
distint hæt sies sjynin

apo dir saat-leddirt skiejins,
d'ir ay lævin sumquhar.

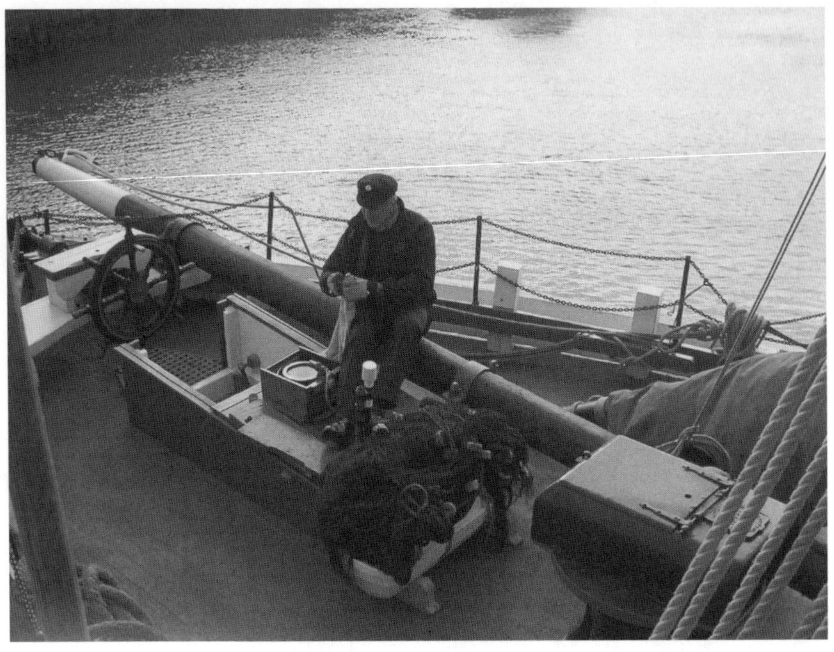

To come back safe, or not, from the sea brought the world home to them.

The sea's the way the world comes to us. Has the boat come in?

Nearly every house had a merchant seaman in it, a father, an uncle, a son,

gathering strange little bits of the broad world and all its foreign tongues for folk to gawk at.

Men, gone for a couple of years, that reappear, mysterious, distant hot seas shining

on their salt-leathered skin, they're permanently leaving somewhere.

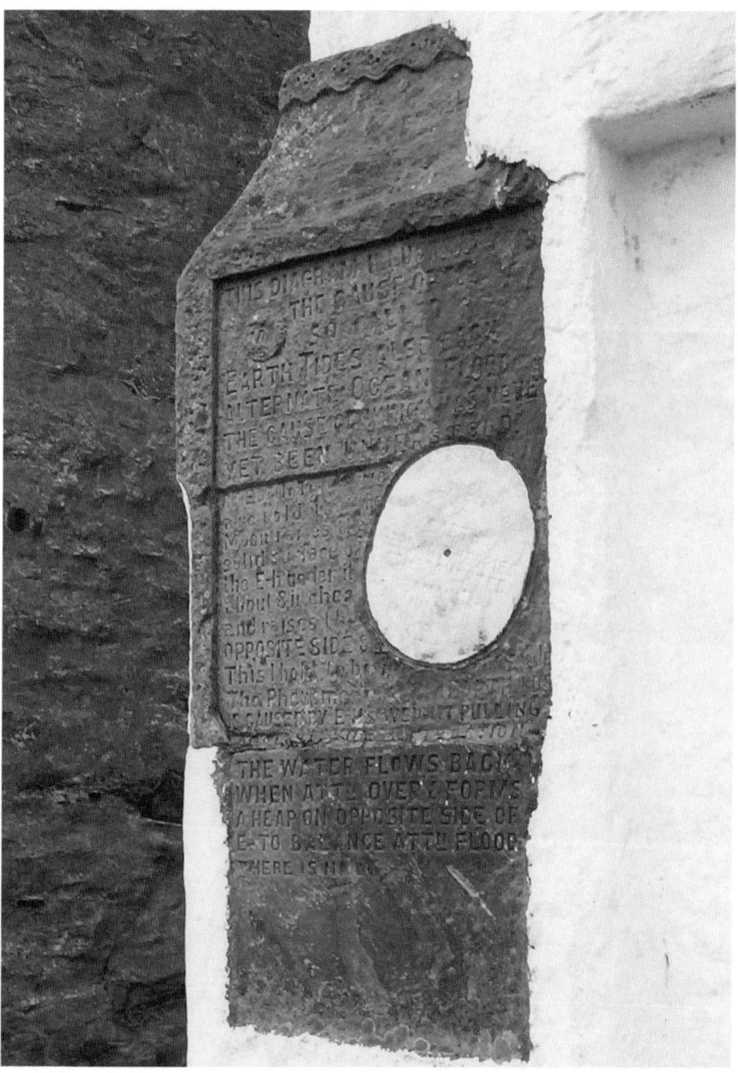

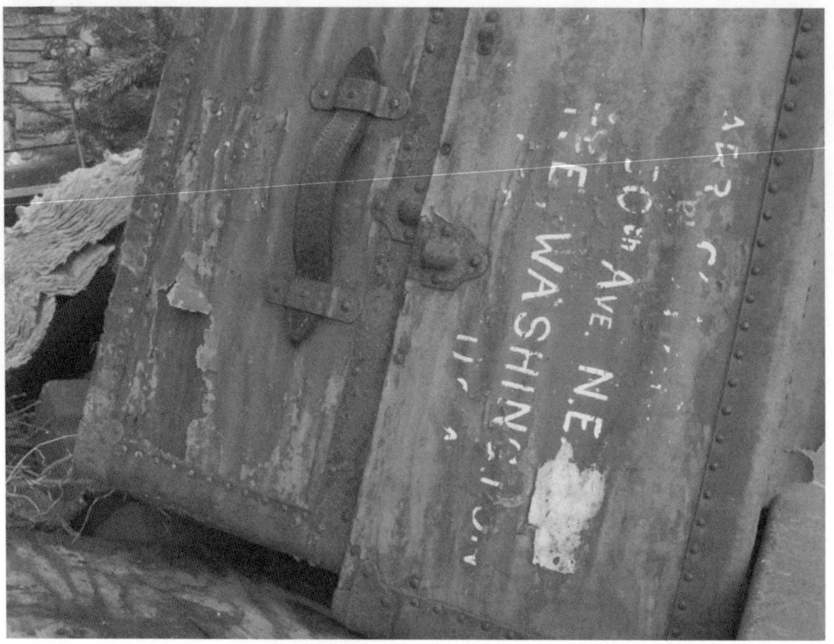

TO COMPASS

The knowledge, understanding and artifacts of the world that the merchant seamen brought home with them meant that although Shetland was a small isolated community in global terms, its folk had an awareness of the true size of the world. This demonstrates the misapprehension that such a 'marginal' community is less informed about the world at large than more 'central', metropolitan situations, where everything, it appears, is near at hand. The habit of looking out, of watching the horizon (both literal and metaphorical) is established early in a sea-faring community, seeking to 'compass' the world. The Latin origin of the word means 'to measure, to make a circuit of'.

TA KOMPIS

Dæ kerriet da surfæs roondnis,
da brædth a'da wirld,
ati'da globbs a'dir heds.

Da cherts a'dir herts
led dim hem, læk doos –
an ungkinnis kam wie dim.

Pietir a'da Blikk shaain fokk
his fotoos a'da
Tokjo Olimpiks.

Alik Pietirsin's brod grin
kinfjoosin dim, diskrybin dim
krossin da Intirnashnil Dæt Lyn?

An Ungkil Alan, wirsit-kæpt
wie gun in haand, haddin da tæil
o a harpoont quhæl.

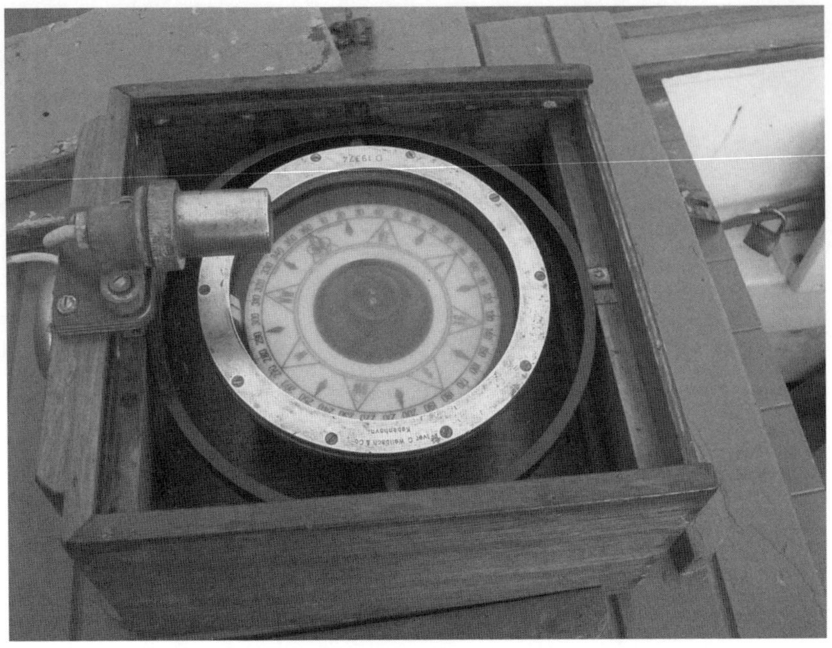

They carried the full surface roundness, the breadth of the world, in the globes of their heads.

The charts of their hearts led them home, like doves – and strangeness came with them.

Peter of the Blick showing folk his photos of the Tokyo Olympics.

Alec Peterson's broad grin confusing them, describing his ship crossing the International Date Line?

And Uncle Alan, woollen-capped with gun in hand, holding the tail of a harpooned whale.

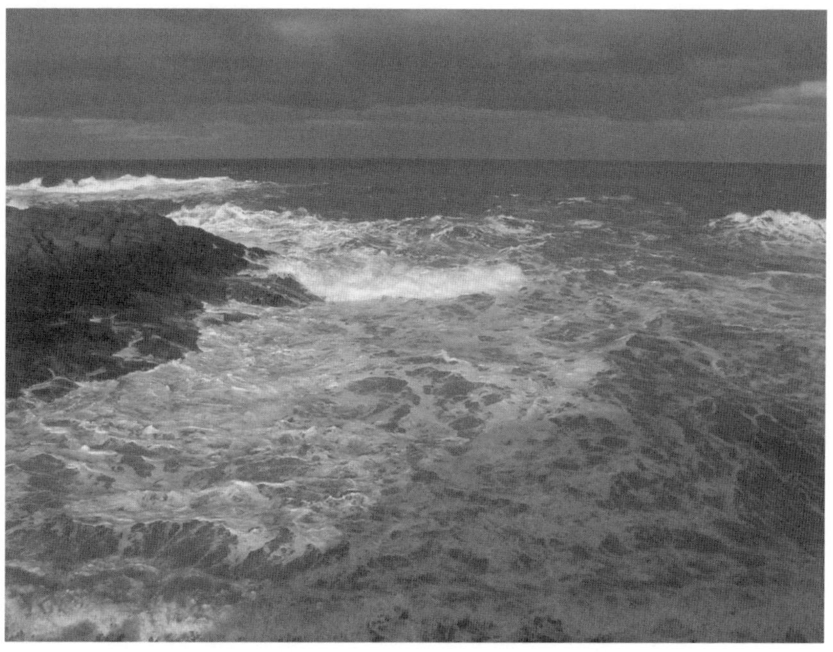

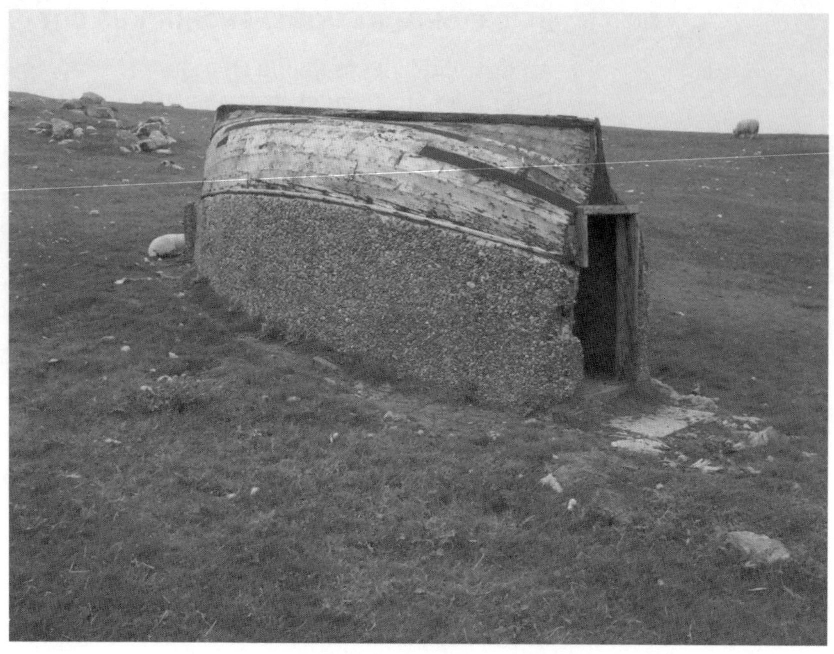

THE DAY JIM HAWKINS' ENGINE CUT OUT

The family name of Hawkins, with its *Treasure Island* and Spanish Armada connotations, was brought to Sandness by the much-loved Church of Scotland missionary, the Reverend Cecil Hawkins, some of whose children subsequently settled there, making Hawkins now very much a 'Saanis' name. The 'Bobbie' of this poem is my grand-uncle, the late Bobbie Garrick, a famous local wit who took his pleasure teasing the customers at the village shop he latterly worked in.

DA DÆ CHIM HAAKINS' ENCHIN KUT OOT

Ati'da middil a'Papa Soond an
Fædir saa him staandin aft,
wævin his jalloo ojilskjin brieks.

Foand da kostgærd,
panikt, a sens a'horrir
as he siemt t'drift

apo da Hum a'Melbie
ati'da ræs a'tyd –
ræl fær aroond.

Dan rielief
as da boat
kliert da krægs

an hædit ootby
t'da opin waatirs
a'Sænt Magnis Bæ.

A pierie start eftir
da Æd lyfboat
pikkit'im up.

'Bettir ös a man
nivir med a'his brieks,'
Bobbie sed.

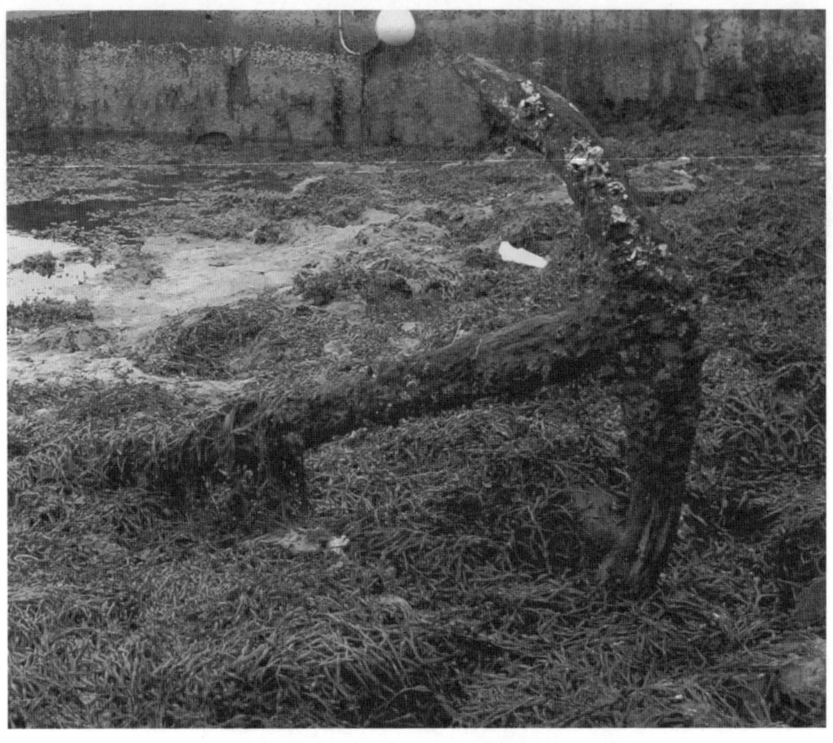

In the middle of Papa Sound and father saw him standing aft, waving
    his yellow oilskin trousers.

Phoned the Coastguard, panicked, a sense of horror as he seemed to
    drift

upon the Holm of Melby in the rush of tide – real fear around.

Then relief as the boat cleared the rocks

and drifted out into the open waters of St Magnus Bay.

A short while later the Aith lifeboat picked him up.

'Better use a man never made of his britches,' Bobbie said.

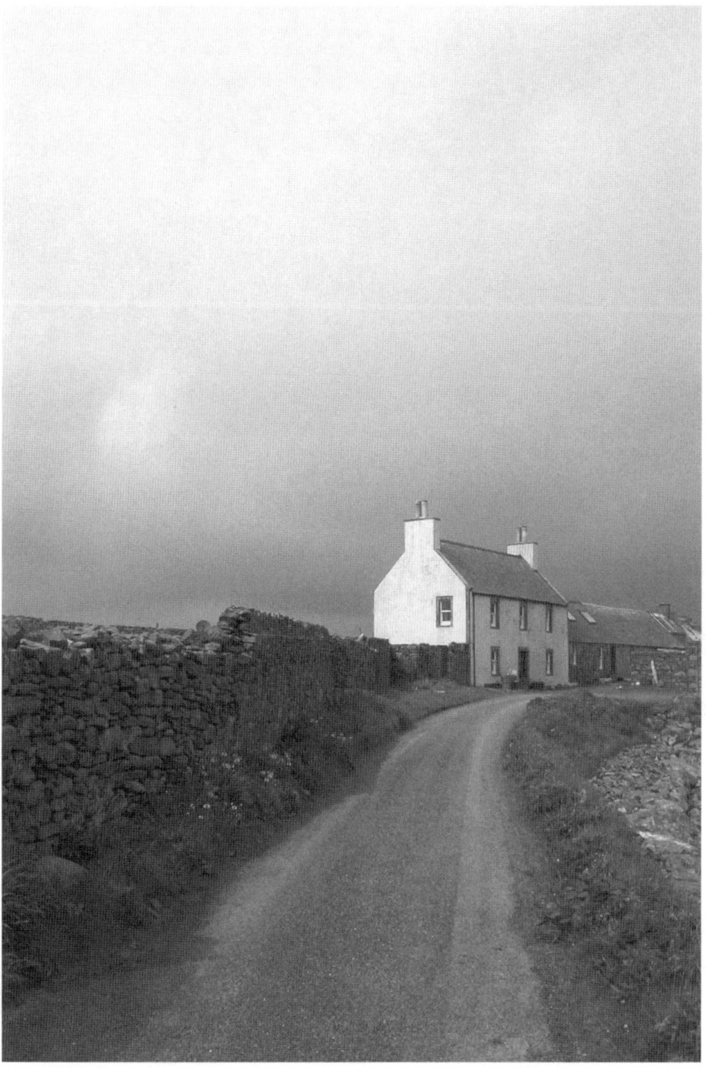

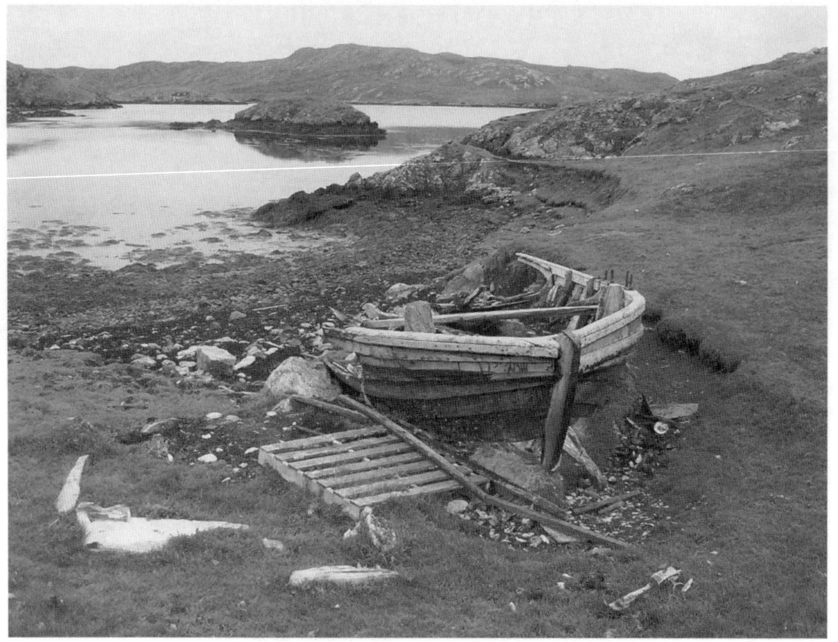

'HIGH SIDE AGAIN, BOYS!'

The story-teller referred to in this poem was also named Robert Jamieson, but as with the schoolteacher, he was no relation to me. The change from the patronymic naming system in the 18th century meant that anyone whose father's first name was James became a Jamieson, making genealogy, known locally as 'reddin (combing) kin', a fascinating study full of false leads. This Robert Jamieson, Bobby a'Haa, was a merchant seaman in his youth and had brought a wife home from Middlesborough. They lived in the former landowner's 18th century house, 'Da Aald Haa' – the old hall – at the head at the Melby pier, next to the more imposing, newer 'Mukkil Haa' – the Big Hall – where the last of the Sandness lairds, the Scotts of Melby, lived until he lost the estate at the end of the 19th century.

'HY SYD AGEN, BOJIES!'

Bobbie a'da aald Haa,
his mukkil oobin laagh boosin lugs,
tells agen his best-kent tæl.

Aboot da kroo a'laandlubbirs
ran in atill a hævie swaal,
an quhan dir boat biegan

t'pitch an rowl, dæ ran
fæ port t'starboard,
fæ starboard bakk t'port,

t'try an kiep a lævil dæk.
Da showt gied up – 'Hy syd agen, bojies!'
'Hy syd agen!'

He tinks – Ja, choost læk wis fokk
t'gjing skuttrin ers first,
tinkin'it wir døin ryght

quhyl we makk wirsels siek.
An quhan we ken w'ir wirkit dirt
we wiss t'Gød we hedna,

bit winna aain da wrakk w'ir med
biekaas we klem we kent næ bettir.

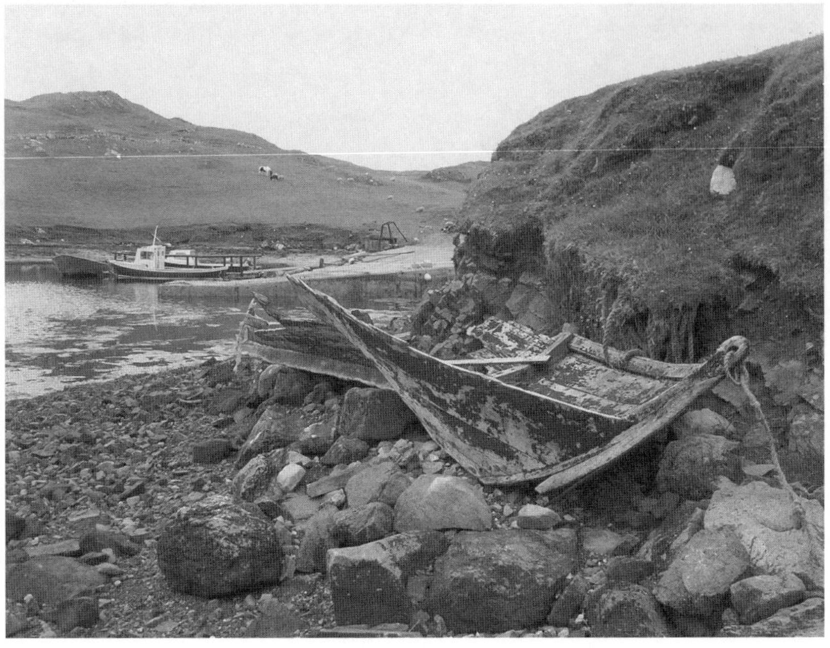

Bobbie from the old Hall, his great hooting laugh buffeting ears, tells
    again his favourite story.

About a crew of landlubbers who ran into a heavy swell, and when the
    boat began

to pitch and roll, they ran from port to starboard, from starboard
    back to port,

trying to nullify the motion. The shout went up – 'High side again,
    boys! High side again!'

He thinks – Just like us people, that, getting things back to front,
    thinking that we're doing right

while we make ourselves ill. And when we realise our folly we wish to
    God we hadn't,

but won't accept the blame for damage because we claim we knew no
    better.

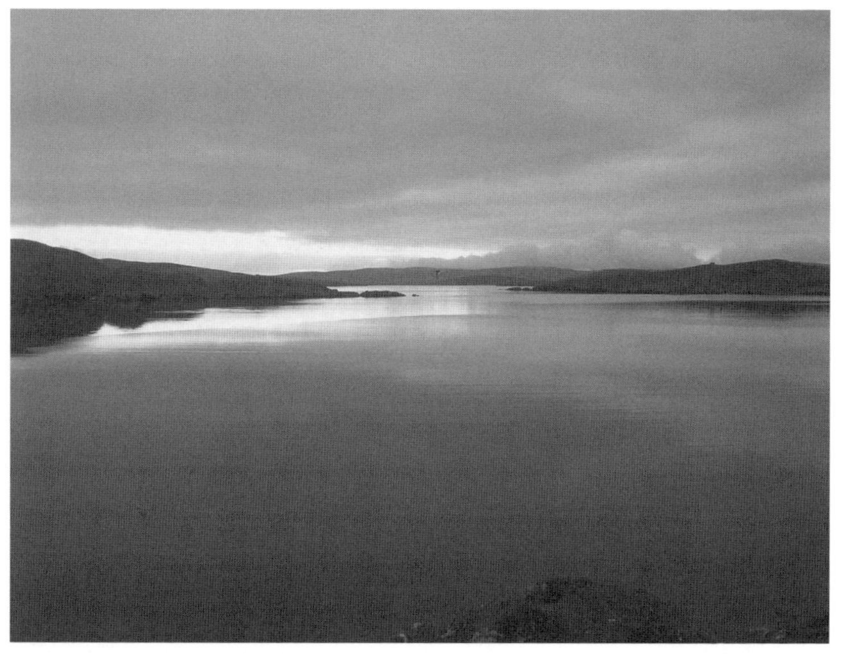

III

ATLANTIK MARIEN

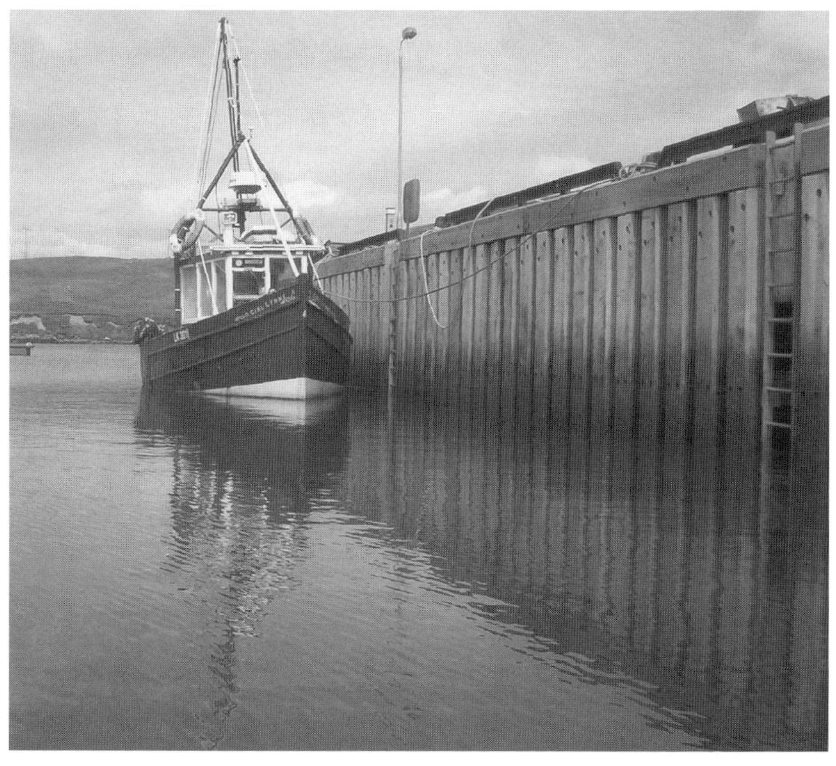

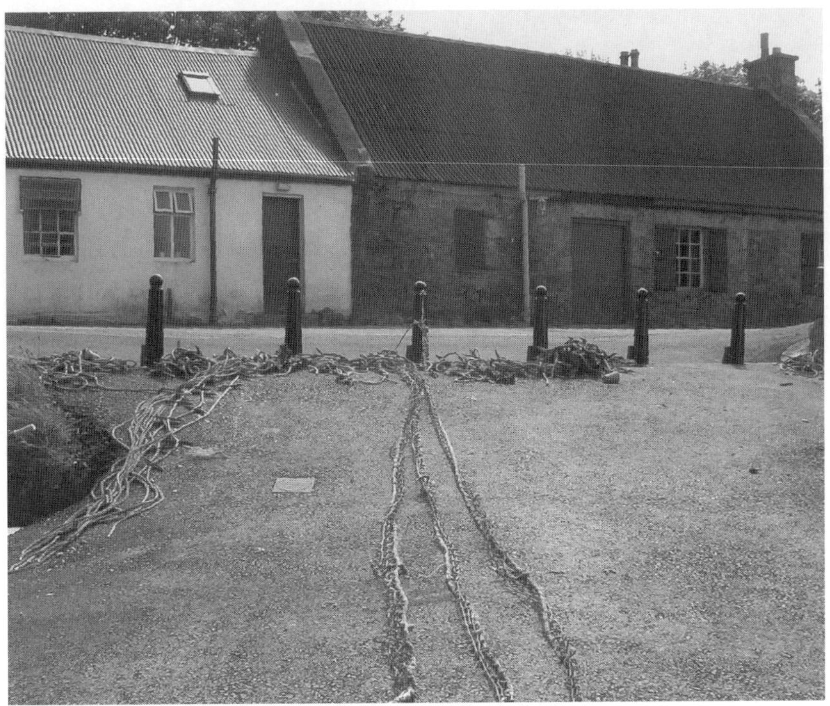

ASHORE

The commonality of ocean binds nationalities, so the culture of the seafront is an international one and once disconnected from locality, the sailor settles wherever work is to be found. For Shetlanders, this meant the establishment of little 'immigrant ghettos' in all the main ports of Britain, and some far beyond, where local traditions were kept alive for a generation or so by means of events such as Up-Helly-Aa celebrations or dances with 'reestit mutton' suppers. But even these land-based events become alien to the sailor. He steps from the vessel to find that it is the land which is swaying and floating, and that 'his people' are not an ethnic grouping, but those who share a way of life.

ASHOAR

He klyms,
jalloo ojil-skiejin flaapin,
fæ da loa-tyd berth.

Skæls apo his skaars,
swæt an drizzil
trikkilin trow aa.

Da pieir swæjies, unjieldin,
rubbir bøt soals piestir
trow a diesil puddil.

Da bar doar swings opin,
bar floar tyls katsh a slop –
waatir amung waatirie fiet.

Mooths stræn t'fin
a gless, a smyl,
a friendlie wird.

Da roar a'da bojies at da dartboard
ekkoas da roar a'da inboard,
an hit's fyn t'ken

da wirld is still aflot.

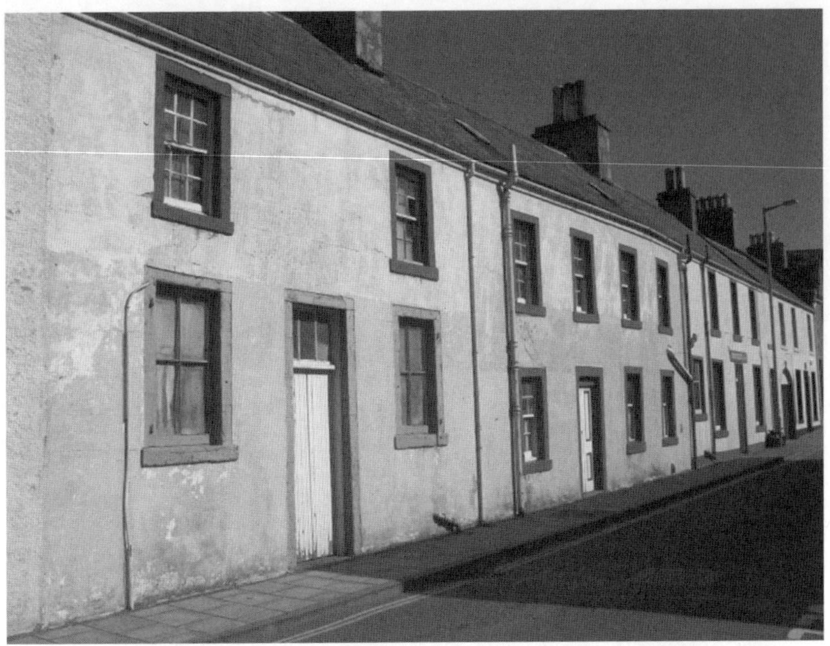

He climbs, yellow oilskin flapping, from the low-tide berth.

Scales on his scars, sweat and drizzle trickling through everything.

The pier sways, unyielding, Wellington bootsoles whisper through a
    diesel puddle.

The bar door swings open, bar floor-tiles catch a slop – water among
    watery feet.

Mouths strain to find a glass, a smile, a friendly word.

The roar of the boys around the dartboard echoes the roar of the
    inboard, and it's good to know

the world is still afloat.

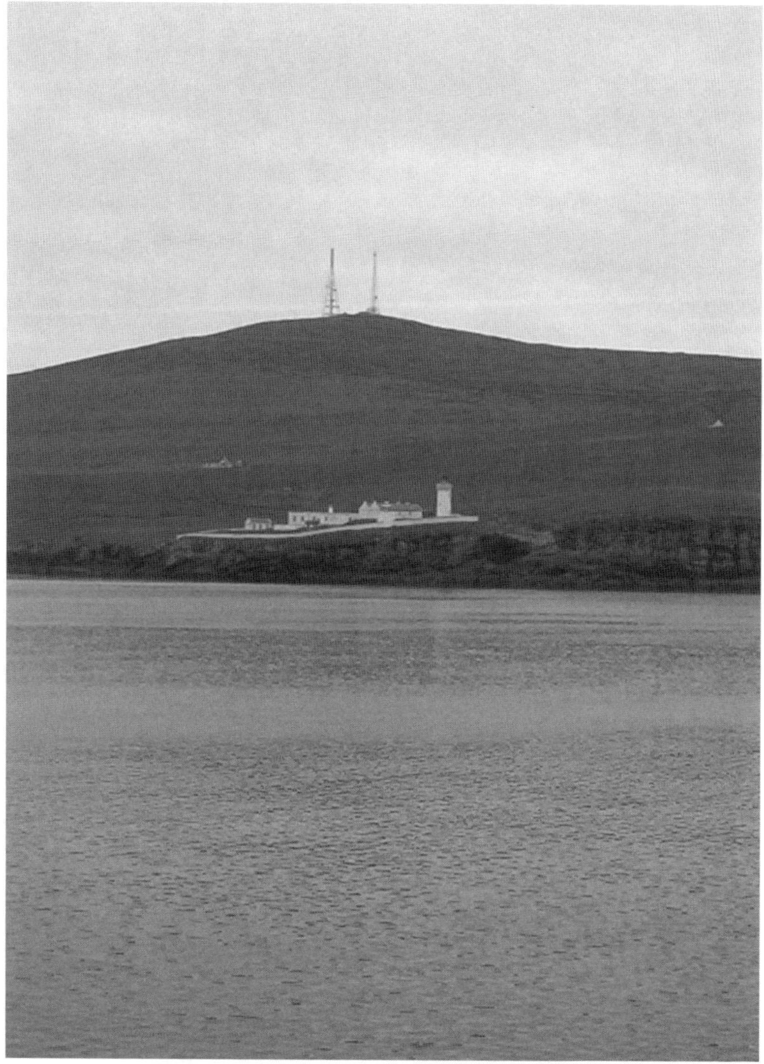
PAGE 94

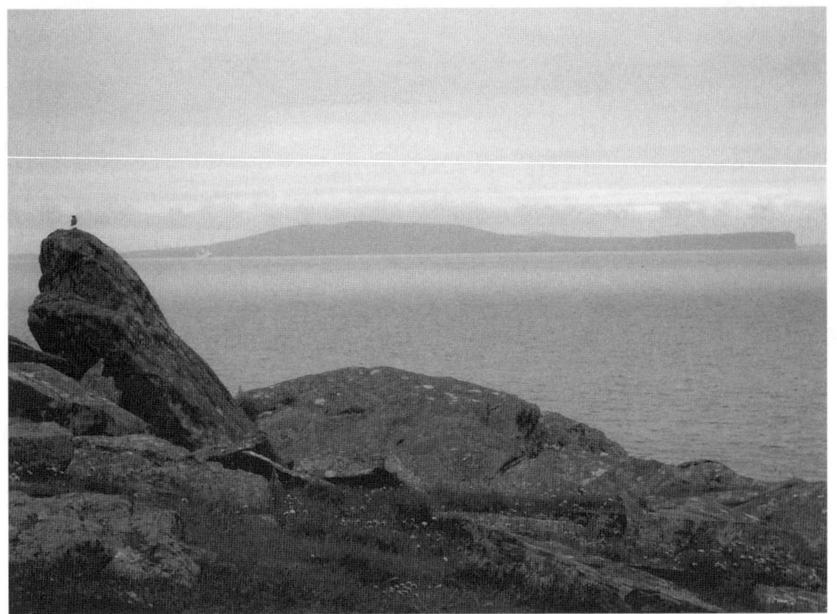

A PORTHOLE ON THE WORLD

Two of Shetland's finest musicians are honoured here – the late Willie Hunter, whose 'Leaving Lerwick Harbour' is now a classic tune; while the reference to 'slokkit' light refers to the late great Eshaness fiddler, Muckle Tammie Anderson, who almost single-handedly sparked a revival in the traditional fiddle music of the islands that continues to flourish today – and whose lament for the death of the world of his youth in Eshaness he entitled 'Da Slokkit Licht'. But this poem suggests that new light illuminates that darkness. The porthole on the ship that carries us away from the familiar brings new sights, new colours, as the vessel steams on. Originally an opening in the side of a ship for exit and entrance of cargo, later the apertures in a ship of war through which cannons were pointed, now the porthole serves solely for the admission of light and air – and by analogy, wisdom.

A PORT HOL APO DA WIRLD

Lerook's lyghts ir slokkit,
da Bard, da Noup a'Noss,
dan Sumbra Hed faa oot a'syght.

Skootiealin's skiejiff da swaall.
Dir noght bit kirnin oshin
aa aroond'im.

Da wirld is swaarmin noo,
a waatirie grind is opnin t'da suddirt,
t'lat a njoo lyght in.

A diffrint lyght aatagiddir,
an en'at døsna chænch wie sæsins,
bit hadds its koors trowoot da jieir.

Tropiekil hæt an fremmit mæt,
boannie broon skiejind laassis,
owirgjing da toght a'hem.

Tæn fæ da toons, he'll gjing
quhar he mann gjing tae,
dø quhit he mann dø.

Hadd doon his dennir.
settil sumwy, in a port.
Wirk an liv.

Læiev.

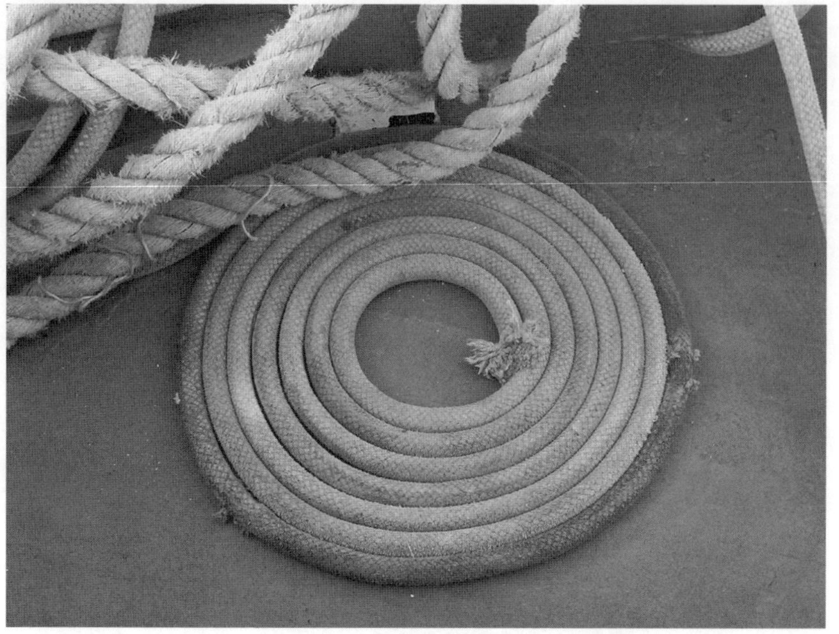

Lerwick's lights are extinguished, the cliffs of Bressay and of Noss, then Sumburgh Head fall out of sight.

Birds of the open seas swoop the swelling water. There's nothing but churning ocean all around them.

The world is swinging now, a watery gate is opening southwards, to let a new light in.

A different light altogether, and one that doesn't change with seasons, but holds its course throughout the year.

Tropical heat and foreign food, beautiful brown-skinned girls, dominate the thought of home.

Removed from the familiar place, he'll go where he must go to, do what he must do.

Stop himself from being seasick. Settle somewhere in a port. Work and live.

Leave.

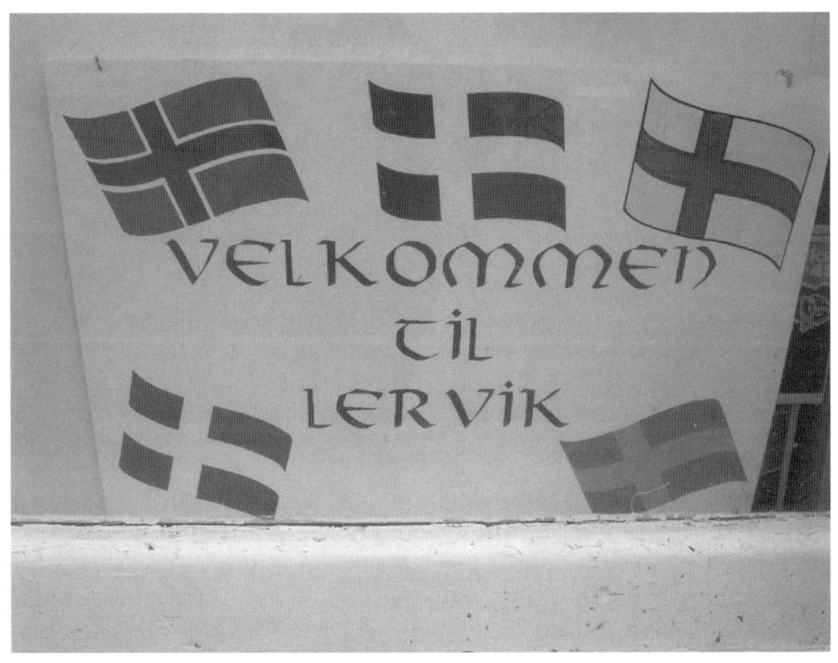
VELKOMMEN
TIL
LERVIK

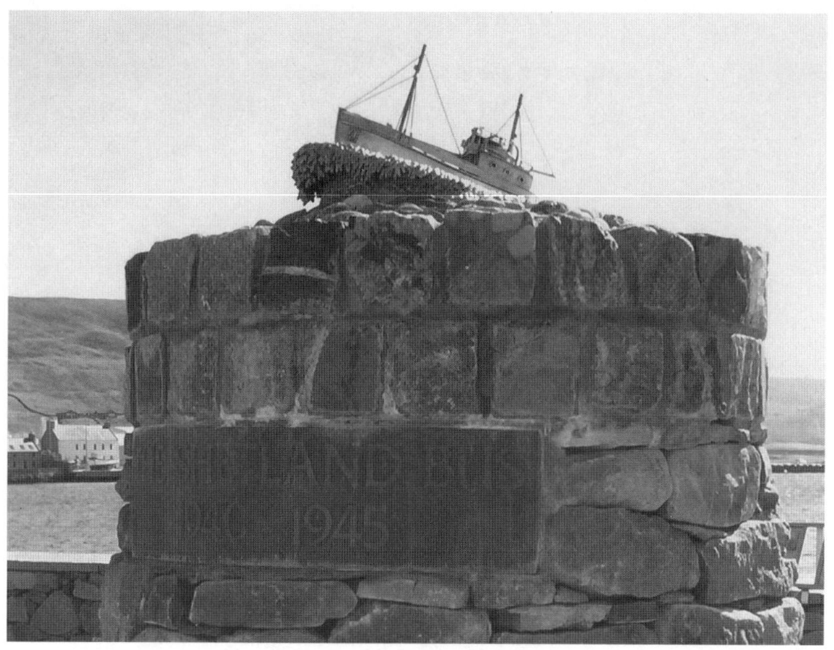

FROM THE WEST (NORWEGIAN)

The axis north to south, to and from Scotland, has been the Shetlanders' main trade route for centuries now, mirroring the political shift away from Scandinavia. With the exception of the wartime 'Shetland Bus' which ran regular and dangerous trips to Norway in fishing boats to sabotage Nazi activities, the journey eastwards to Norway, though historically important, has been much less travelled in recent times. But in the late 20th century, the establishment of new sea and air networks in the post-oil North Sea has revived these links. And of course there were always the merchant seamen whose work carried them to these shores, approaching Norway 'from the west', who recognised there the familiar language of home.

VESTENFRAA

He gied t'sæl
da Norrowa kost,
kerrjin kargo

nort an sooth,
in an oot trow
fjord an fell.

Færd at first
ta opin his mooth,
till he startit t'hieir

a lokk a'wirds
he toght he kent
wis spokkin hieraboots.

'Sjetlandsk,' sæs he,
dyghtin himsel –
'Sjetlandsøyene.'

An dæ nod dir heds,
da Norskies, an wie a'kynd
a'Sjaetlin soond, sæ 'Ja.'

He tinks –
Jeg kjenner min fokk –
Wir æin fokk.

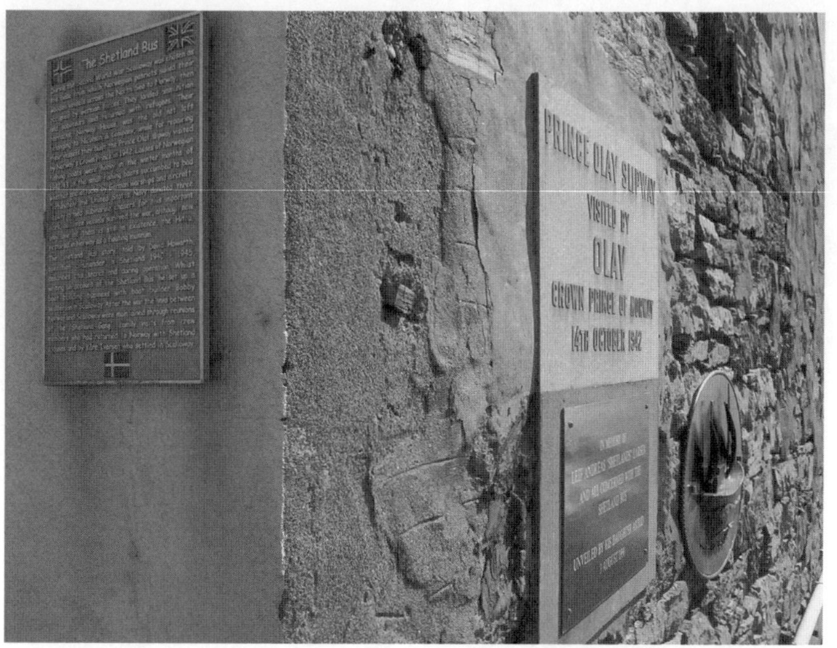

He went to sail the Norway coast, carrying cargo
north and south, in and out through fjord and fell.
At first timid about speaking out loud, he began to hear
a store of words he thought he knew were spoken there.
'Shetlander,' he says, indicating himself – 'The Shetland Islands.'
And they nod their heads, the Norwegians, and with a Shetlandic
    accent, say 'Yes.'
He thinks – I recognise my company – our own people.

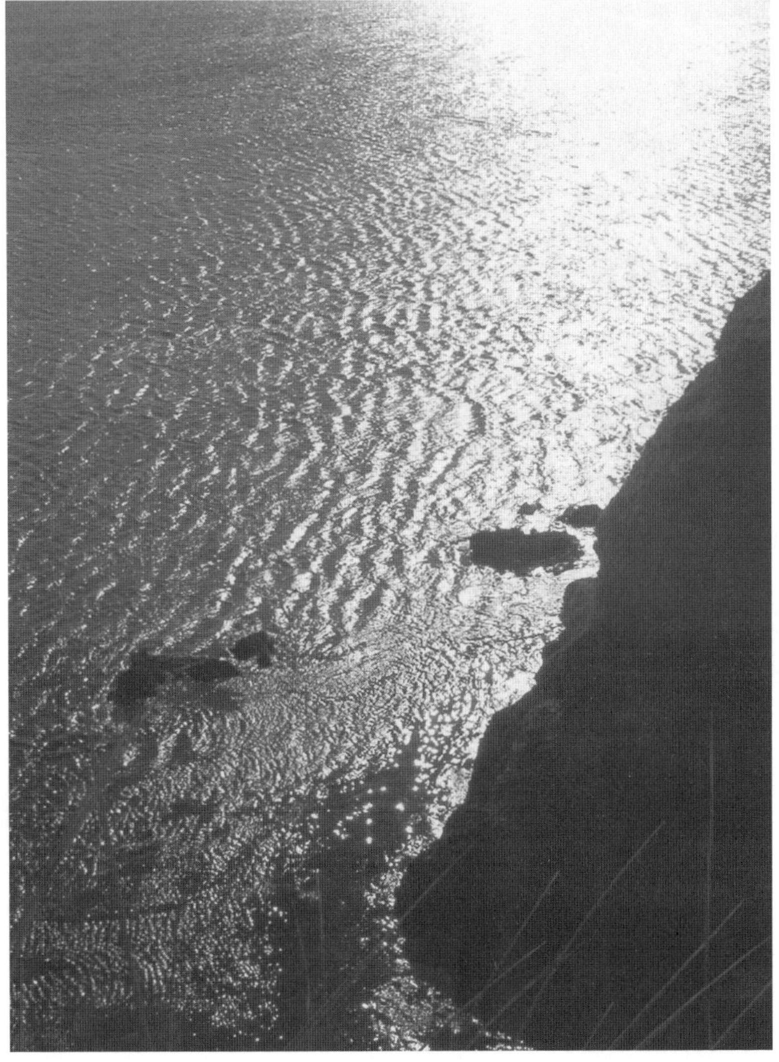

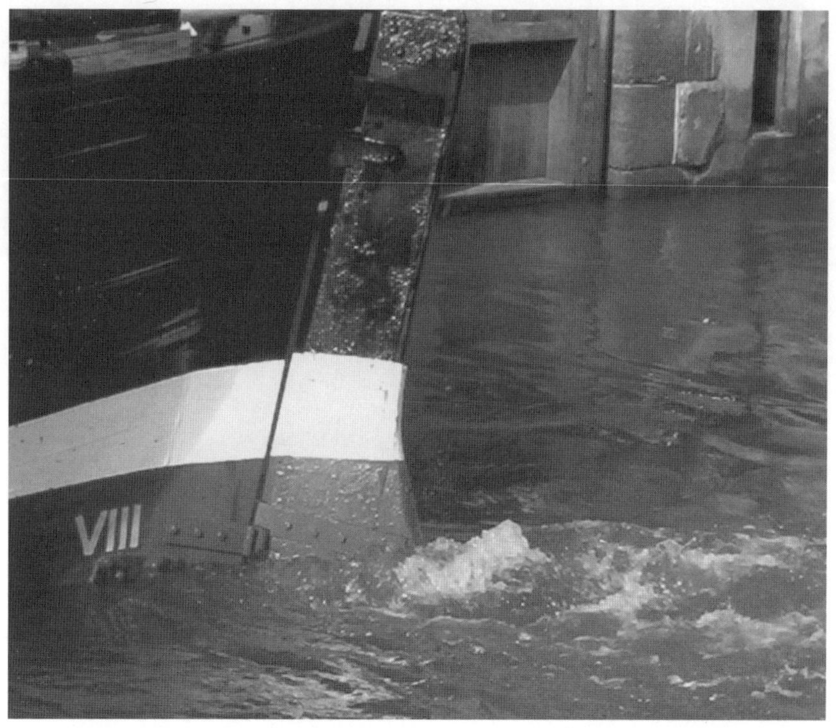

LOST BUOY

Innocence is soon eroded by exposure to life at sea. Some are less 'able seamen' than others – the ability to float doesn't necessarily entail a direction. Disconnected from the rope that bound it, the buoy drifts, waiting for someone to haul it from the water, to give it purpose.

LOST BOW

He's gien owir far oot –
quhieir dat, fir sumien
startit sæ far oot ati'da iddir

direkshin aatagiddir.
Bit quhit wid he mynd a'dat noo,
jun pierie laad apo a skerrie?

Dan he wis bit a toght-trævlir,
kiepin t'da shoormil,
dræmin a'ootby.

Admyrin da siemin's tan
an windrin, windrin
da koors dæ sælt.

Bit noo his sjip's kum in,
uppit angkir, gien an drappt him
apo a ungkin pier,

in a ungkin toon,
in a ungkin kuntrie,
an æsie pikk-up fir da hoors.

Desprit fir passiech hem,
an emtie bunk, he takks
a koarn a'komfirt dær.

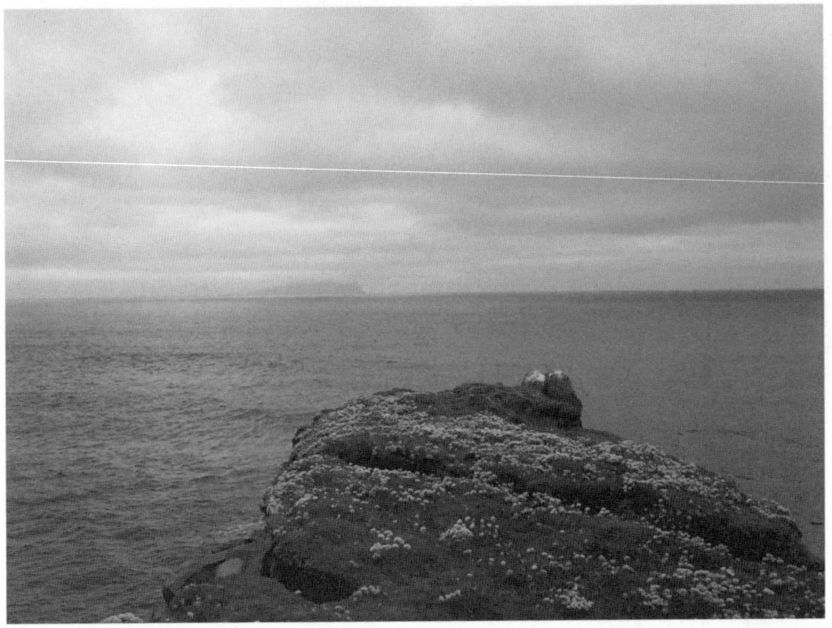

He's gone too far out – strange that, for somebody who started so far out in the other

direction altogether. But what would he remember now of that, that little boy upon a skerry?

Then he was just a thought-traveller, keeping to the shallows, dreaming of out there.

Admiring the seaman's tan and wondering, wondering what course they sailed.

But now his ship's come in, upped anchor, gone and dropped him on a foreign pier,

in a foreign town, in a foreign country, an easy pick up for the whores.

Desperate for a passage home, an empty cabin, he finds a little comfort there.

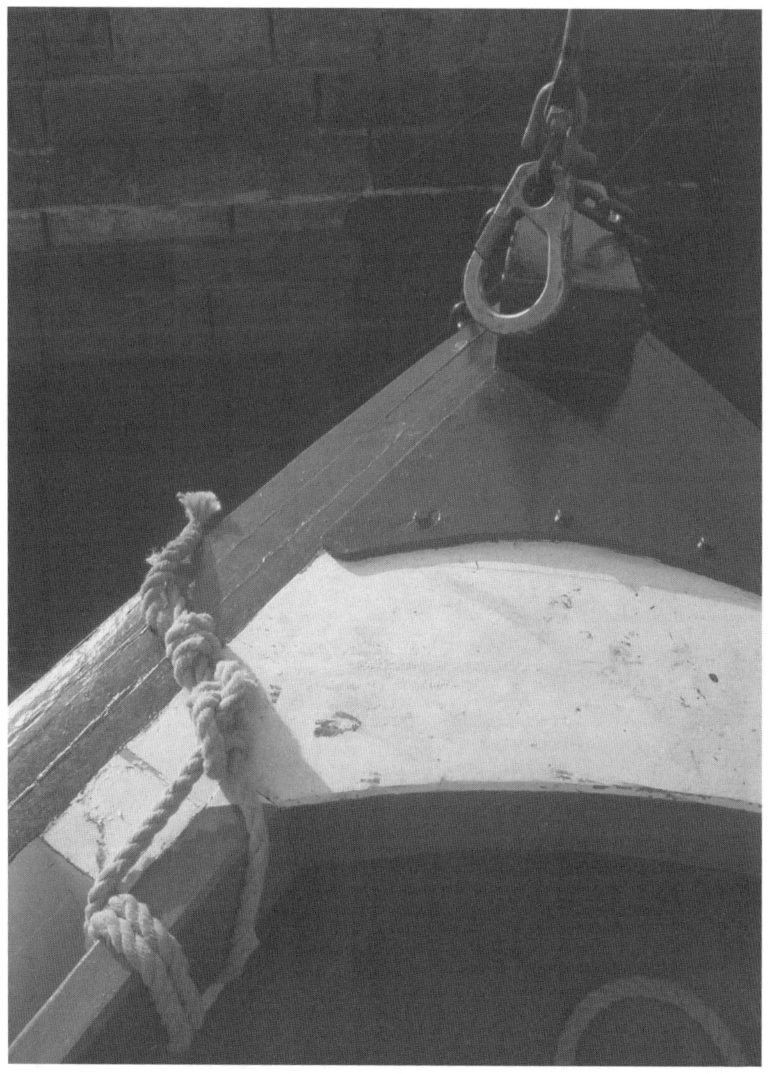

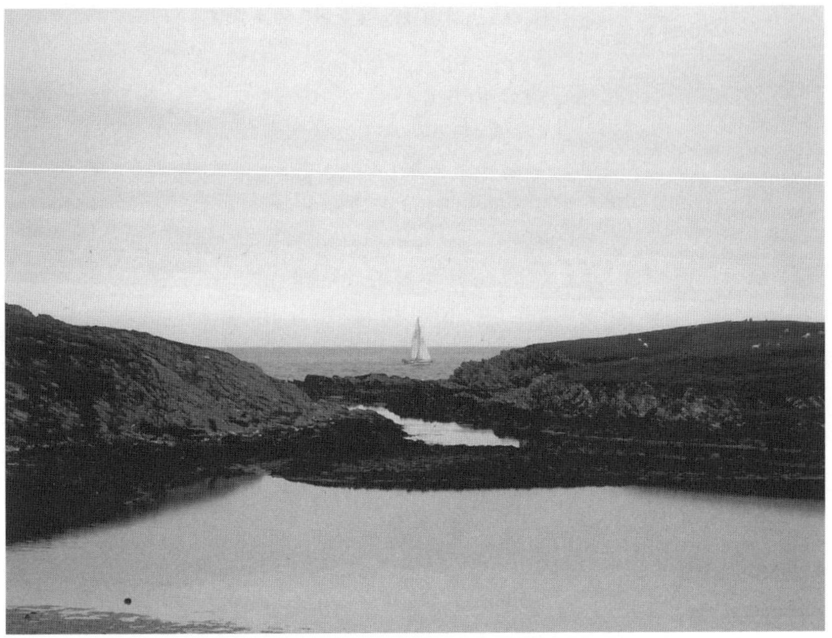

ONLY TRULY AT HOME WHEN AFLOAT

The ship itself becomes the familiar place. In different ports, so many different voices talking, their sound alone insufficient to impart meaning. The solitary sailor learns to keep quiet, observe and learn, as all too often the shore-side erupts with violence. The unexpected springs violently from below the calm surface – but is recognised. The 'doldrums' are a region of the Atlantic around the equator between the North East Trade Winds that blow from north Africa to northern Brazil, and the South Easterlies that blow from Southern Africa to Southern Brazil. The name derives from the Middle English 'dul', sharing its meaning with the Scots word 'dool', or as it is pronounced in Sandness, 'døl' – 'grief' or 'misery'.

ONLIE RYGHT AT HEM AFLOT

A tyd a'ungkin wirds
sirroonds'im
apo da laand.

Evin quhan hit siems kaam,
undirkurrints, tydpøls
draa him in, kepsys him.

Ir dan sylinsis bekaam him,
læv him føshinlis, vyndlis,
adrift ati'da daaldrims.

He looks at da surfies,
quhit siems t'bie soondit
an looks at da mienin:

a wyldnis'at lys a'da depts,
'at da surfies a'lyf
nevir bietræies.

An a kongir eel
kums bummlin
up in a loabstir kriel.

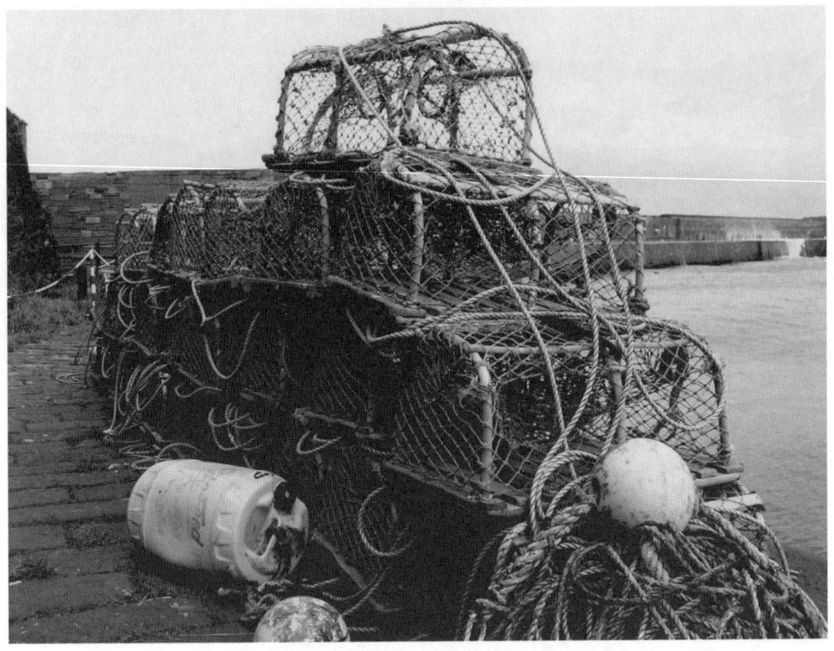

A tide of alien words surrounds him on land.

Even when it seems calm, undercurrents, tidal eddies pull him in, capsize him.

Silences becalm him, leave him powerless, clumsy, adrift in the doldrums.

He looks at the surface, what seems to be sounded and looks at the meaning:

a wildness that lies in the depths, that the surface of life never betrays.

And a conger eel comes up thrashing in a lobster creel.

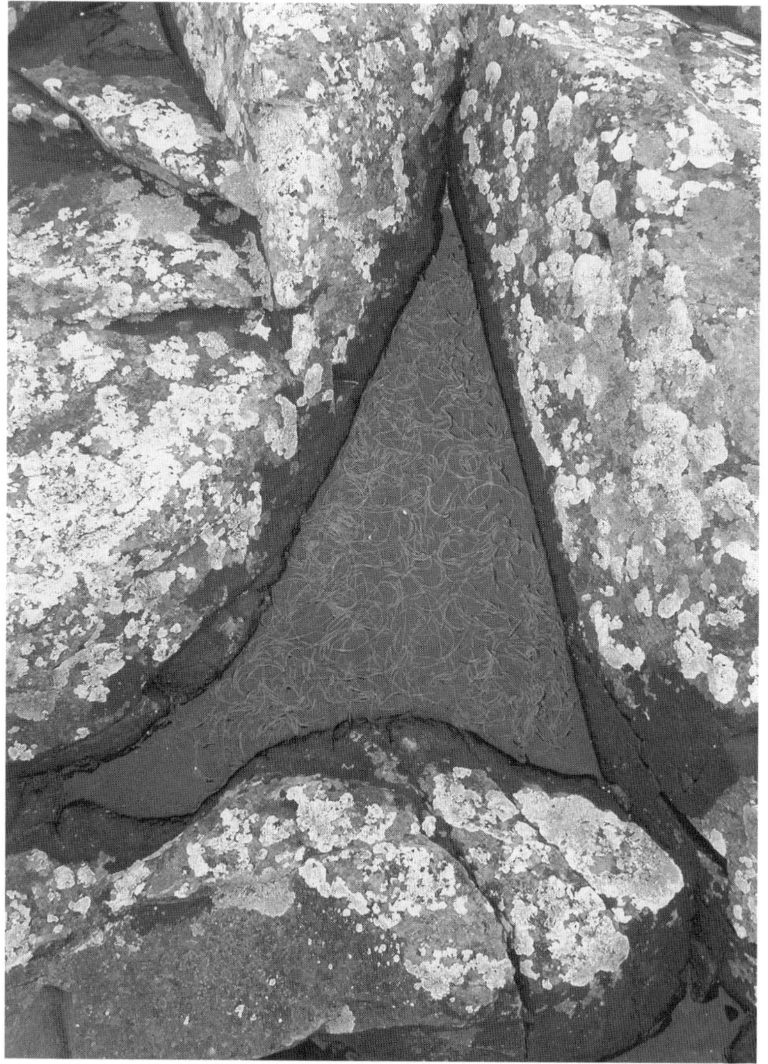

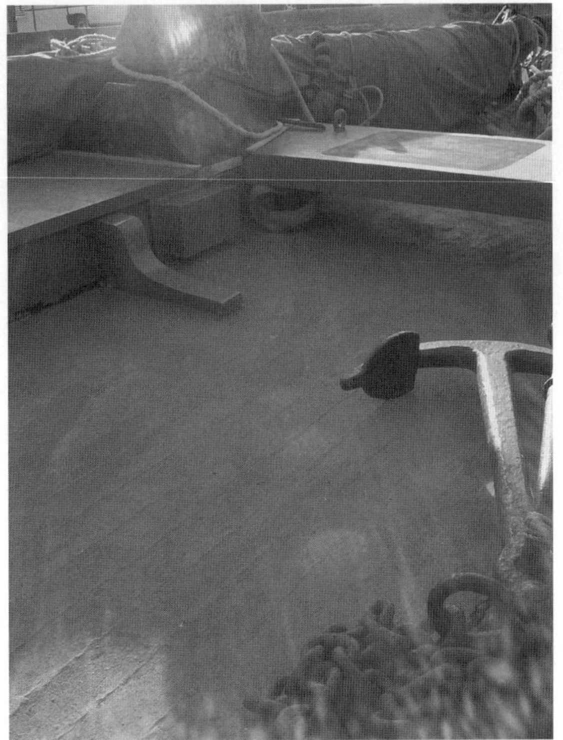

SEA-FARING

The global consciousness that arose from the activities of the sailing men meant that the ocean was never regarded as an obstacle to togetherness, but rather as the means to connect one place with another. The coming of everyday air travel in the latter part of the 20th century has meant that the sea is now regarded differently – though perhaps the learning brought home by the merchant seamen has been replaced, and improved upon, by the new technologies. The moment of enlightenment described by astronauts, when they are able for the first time to look back at our planet and see the beautiful blue ball as a whole for the first time, is not so far removed from the knowledge of those who circumnavigate the world in ships.

SIEVÆGIN

Ajunt da flat ært
a'da boondries a'sens,
he kens –

da wirld's choost
a roond bloo baa fokk sirkil
t'wirk an liv:

a globbil awaarnis.
Du spits ati'da oshin,
a drap myght rekk Æshnis.

Bit hoiest du a sæl,
du gjings quhaar du will,
ta njoo-fun laand.

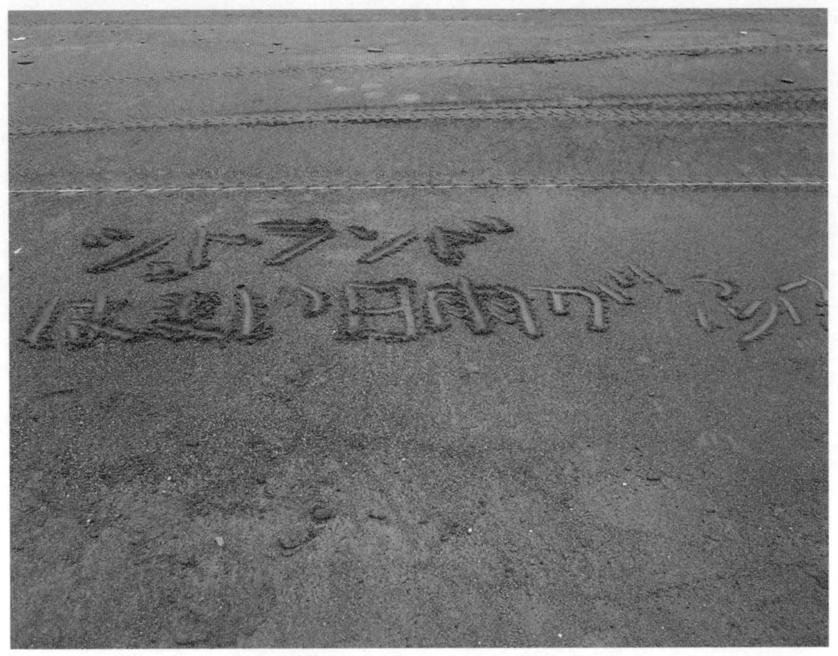

Beyond the flat earth of the boundaries of sense, he knows –

the world is just a round blue ball people circle in order to work and
    live:

a global awareness. If you spit in the ocean, that drop might reach
    Eshaness.

But hoist a sail, and you go where you please, to new found land.

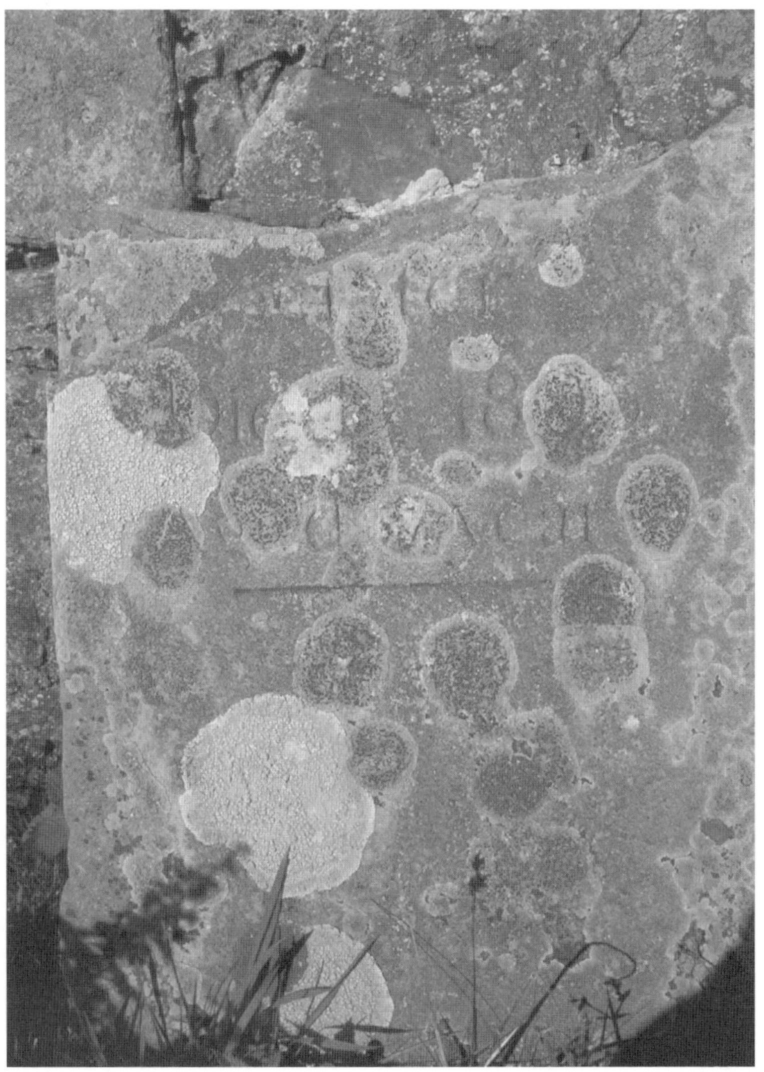

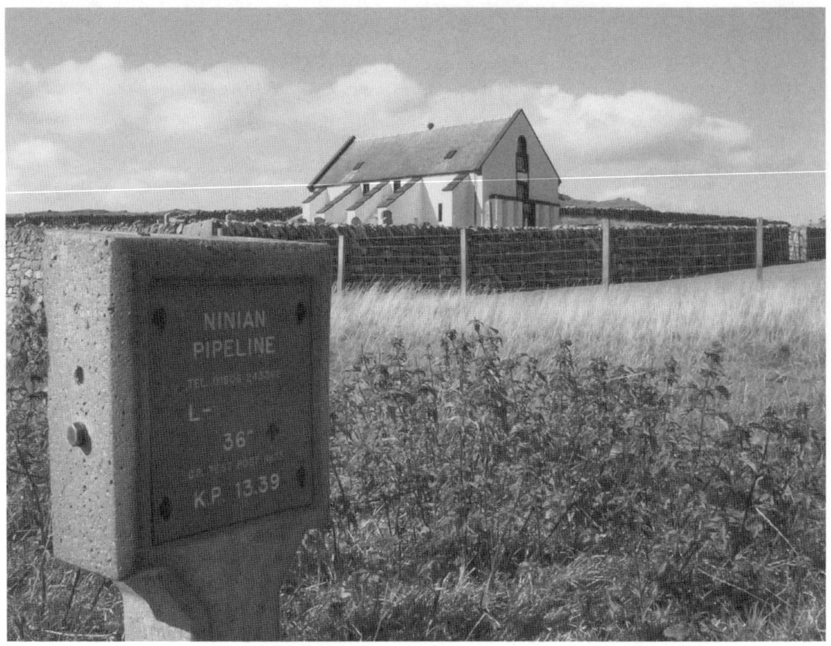

CORACLE

The little wickerwork and leather boats used to voyage the northern seas by the early Christian travellers like St Brendan surely can only have been piloted by faith. Seeking sanctuary away from the distractions of people and their chattering, the Culdees found their retreats in the most unlikely places, guided by a quiet instinct for seeking 'haven'. In a sense, every sea journey is a search for haven, for safe arrival, and a retreat from the land-bound world.

KORIEKIL

He tinks – Gød kens
quheddir du ivir fins hævin.
Du onlie diskuvirs.

Bit dær's monie a hærbir
du tys up a quhyl
in a sjoar-syd myshin.

He tinks – Wirds onlie brakk
læk wæjievs alang biechis
quhar dæ waash up ydieis.

Bit, fæ dum fæth, he trys
ta faashin sum kynd a'kraft
t'lat him gjing sælin

da surfies a'mienin
ta Hievin.

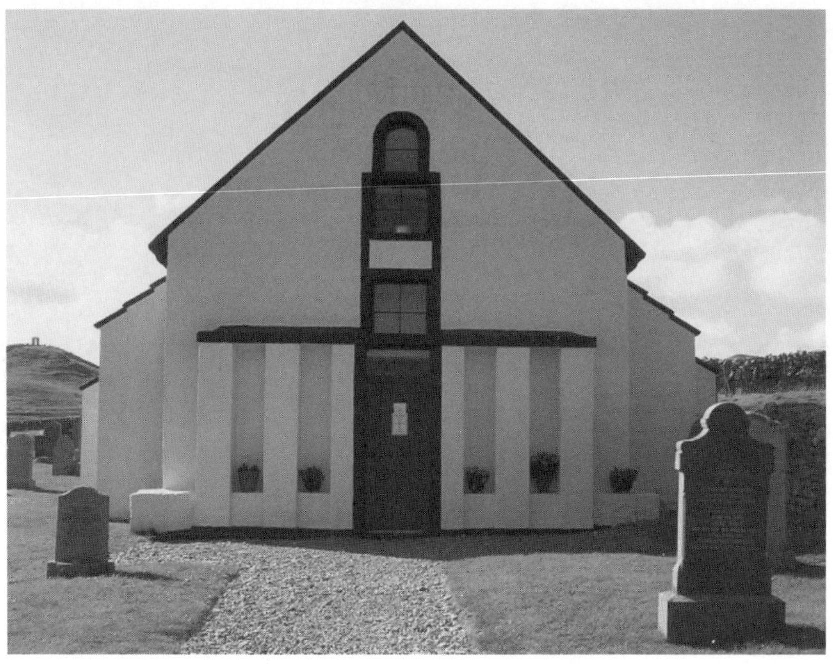

He thinks – God only knows whether you'll ever find haven. You only discover.

But there's many a harbour you tie up a while, in a shore-side mission.

He thinks – Words only break like waves along beaches, where they wash up ideas.

Out of silent faith, he tries to fashion some sort of craft to let him go sailing

the surface of meaning to Heaven.

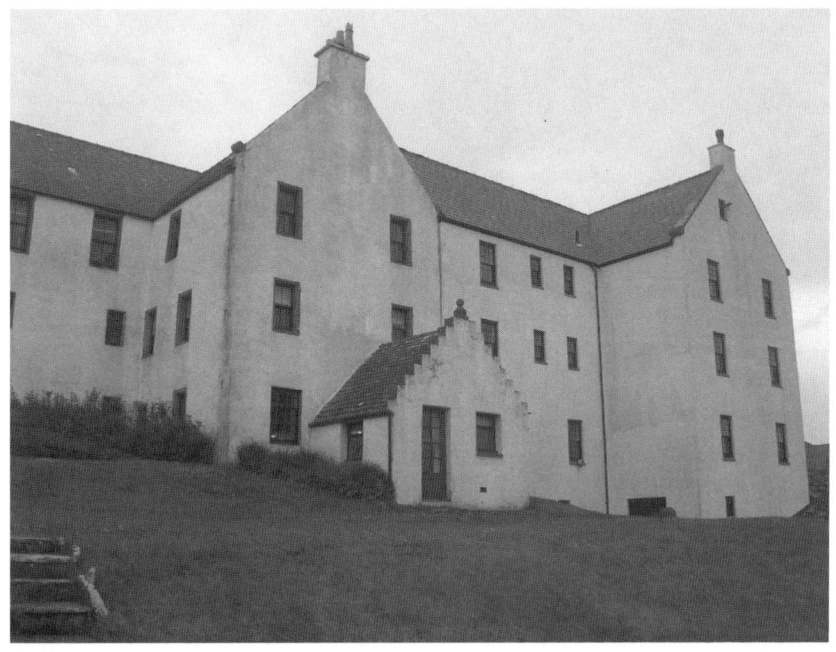

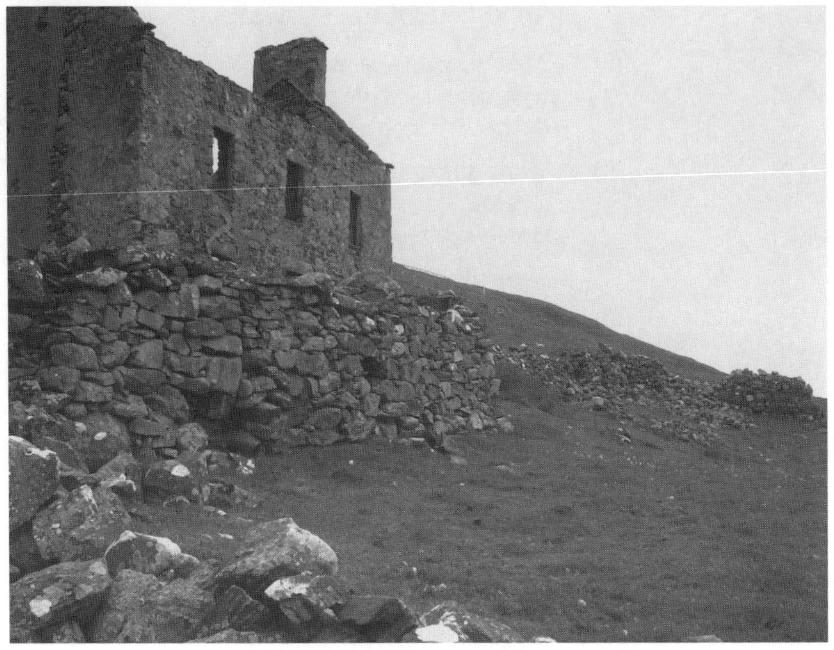

'DO WELL AND PERSEVERE'

The school motto of the Anderson Educational Institute, founded by Arthur Anderson, who started his working life as a 'beach boy' – when he left Shetland to join the Navy, these were the parting words of his employer. Anderson went on to become co-founder of the 'Peninsular & Oriental' shipping line. He was a great benefactor in Shetland in the second half of the 19th century, and in 1847 became the first Member of Parliament for Orkney and Shetland not drawn from the privileged, landed families. He also helped to break the landlords' stranglehold on the fishing industry, assisting crofters in the establishment of their own independent fishing station on the westside island of Vaila.

'DØ WIEL AN PERSIEVIER'

Ahint da aald skøl waa,
tryin smokkin fags,
da mestir's step aroond da koarnir

sends dim spøliejin awa,
riek kummin oot a'mooths,
poochis, girss.

Abøn dir heds, abøn da doar
da mottoo set dær ati'dir herts,
kærvt ati'stæn –

'Dø wiel an persievier.'
Da wirds o Ertie Aandirsin,
an iksampil t'wis aa, dæ sæ,

him at gied an led da foonds
tæ an empyr's pryd an chojie –
da P & O lyn bojie.

He tinks – Na bojies, empyrs næ mær.
Da Merchint Nævie's fieniesht noo.
Gjing ju, ju'll fin næ empyr dær.

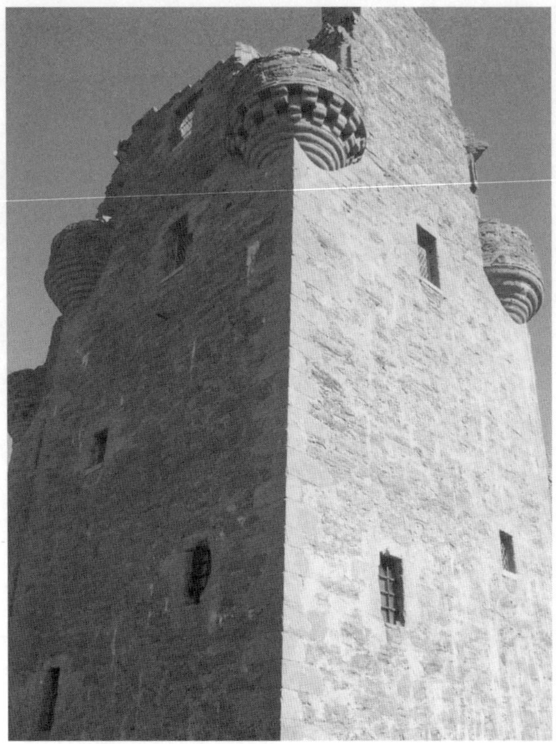

Behind the old school wall, smoking their first fags, the teacher's
step around the corner

sends them scattering away, smoke coming out of mouths, pockets,
grass.

Above their heads, above the door, the motto set there in their hearts
carved in stone –

'Do well and persevere.' The words of Arthur Anderson, an example
to us all, they say,

him that went and laid the foundation of an empire's pride and joy –
the P & O line man.

He thinks – No boys, empires no more. The Merchant Navy's finished
now. Go if you want to, you'll find no empires there.

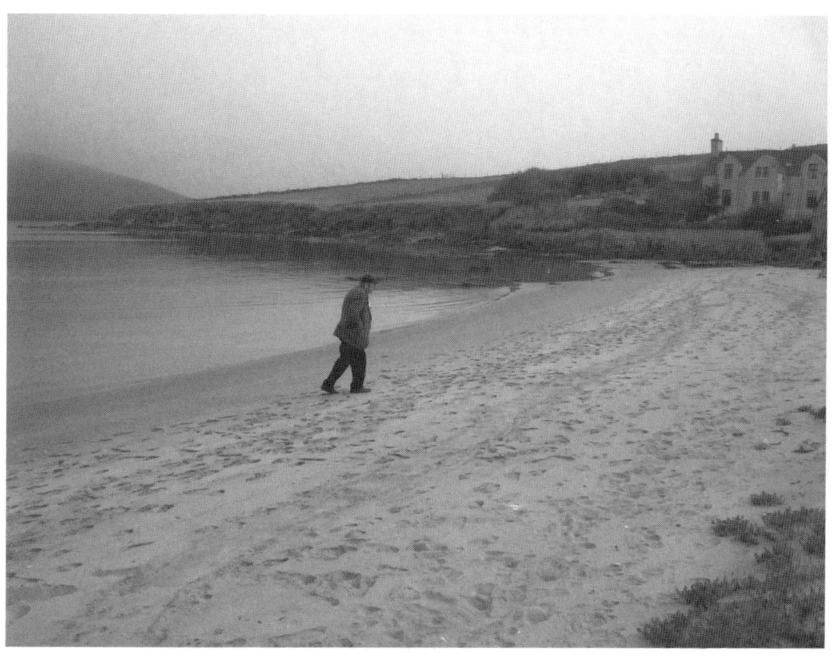

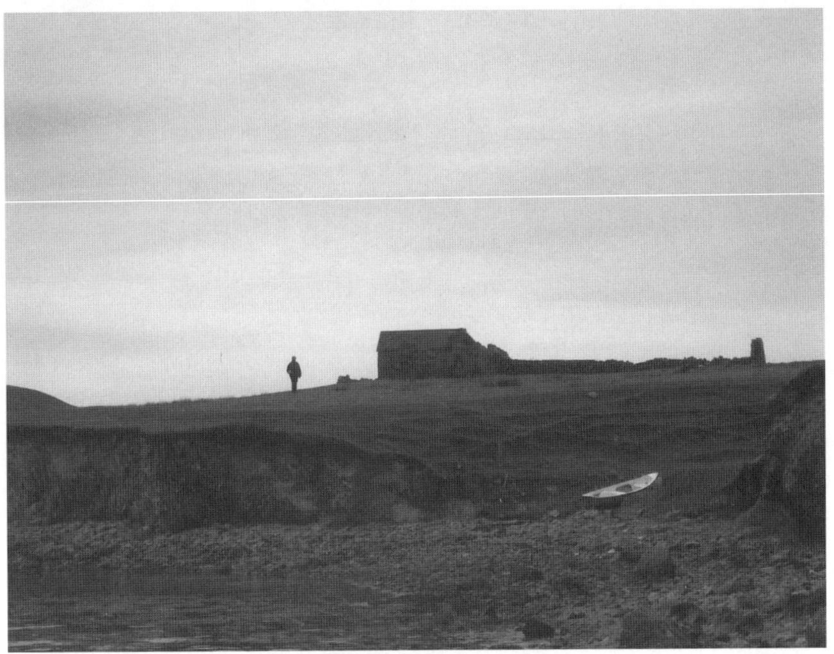

DISABLED SEAMEN

From the time of the Press Gangs during the Napoleonic Wars onwards, Shetlanders joined both the Royal and the Merchant Navies in number, providing every rank from Ordinary Seaman to Admiral. Now the mariner's skills are comparatively redundant and the tradition of 'gjaain t'da sælin' dating back two centuries is largely finished. With it, so the passing of lore from one generation to the next is lost.

DISÆBILT SIEMEN

Dis dæs,
a njoo sylins
faas wie da haar.

He tinks – d'ir næ berth ava.
So he's stoppit tellin
aa da siekrits a'is kraft

t'da kabin bojie
duggin'im,
swaabin'is dæks.

Noo da task is ta mak rædie
a bunk t'læ a lyf-tym apo –
t'fin a sæl-kloot fir a windin-shiet.

He'll byd quhyit
till da wind blaas da haar
fæ da oshin's roar.

Till da sun rippils trow,
he'll hadd'is koonsil kloss.

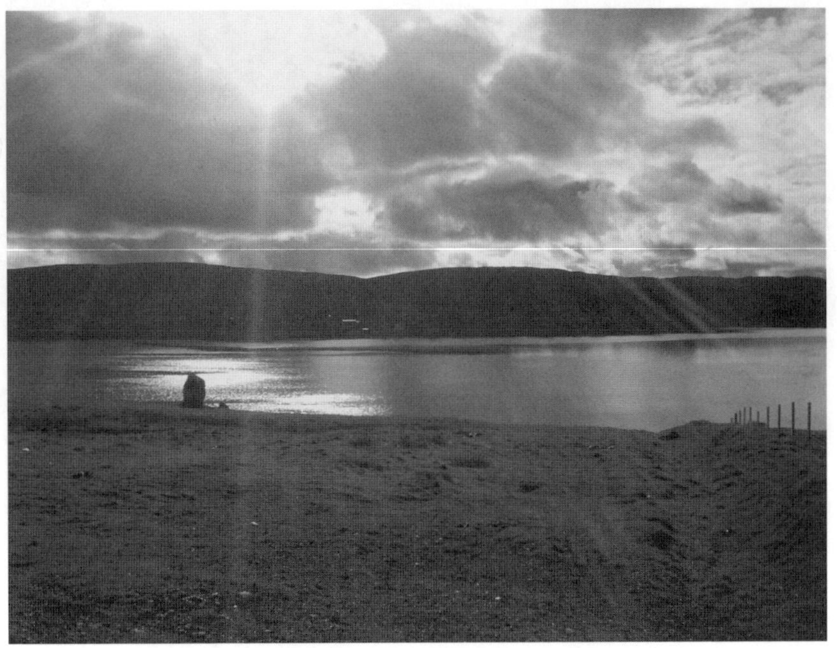

These days, a new silence falls with the sea-mist.

He thinks – There's no work on ships at all. So he's given up telling
the secrets of his craft

to the cabin boy dogging him, swabbing his decks.

Now the task is to make ready a bunk to lay a lifetime on – to find a
sail-cloth for a winding-sheet.

He'll stay quiet till the wind blows the sea mist from the ocean's roar.

Till the sun ripples through, he'll keep his counsel close.

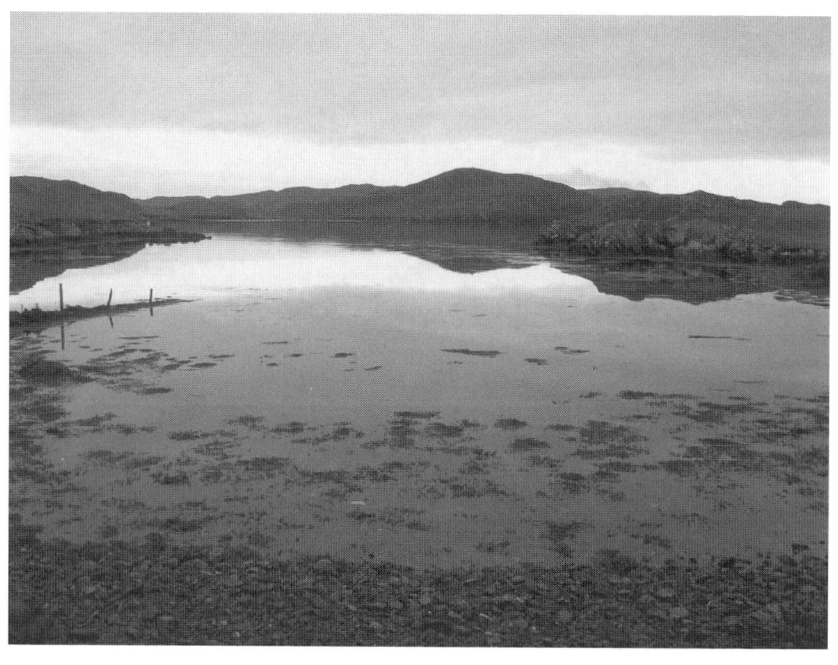

Luath Press Limited
committed to publishing well written books worth reading

LUATH PRESS takes its name from Robert Burns, whose little collie Luath (*Gael.,* swift or nimble) tripped up Jean Armour at a wedding and gave him the chance to speak to the woman who was to be his wife and the abiding love of his life. Burns called one of 'The Twa Dogs' Luath after Cuchullin's hunting dog in Ossian's *Fingal*. Luath Press was established in 1981 in the heart of Burns country, and now resides a few steps up the road from Burns' first lodgings on Edinburgh's Royal Mile.
Luath offers you distinctive writing with a hint of unexpected pleasures.

Most bookshops in the UK, the US, Canada, Australia, New Zealand and parts of Europe either carry our books in stock or can order them for you. To order direct from us, please send a £sterling cheque, postal order, international money order or your credit card details (number, address of cardholder and expiry date) to us at the address below. Please add post and packing as follows: UK – £1.00 per delivery address; overseas surface mail – £2.50 per delivery address; overseas airmail – £3.50 for the first book to each delivery address, plus £1.00 for each additional book by airmail to the same address. If your order is a gift, we will happily enclose your card or message at no extra charge.

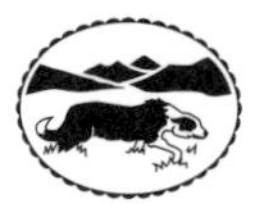

Luath Press Limited
543/2 Castlehill
The Royal Mile
Edinburgh EH1 2ND
Scotland
Telephone: 0131 225 4326 (24 hours)
Fax: 0131 225 4324
email: sales@luath.co.uk
Website: www.luath.co.uk